THE MUTINY
ON BOARD
H.M.S. BOUNTY

THE MUTINY
ON BOARD
H.M.S. BOUNTY
1789

by
William Bligh

Pageminster Press
in association with
Argot Press
&
Mitchell Beazley
1981

All rights reserved. No part of this publication may be reproduced, stored in a retrieval system, or transmitted, in any form or by any means, electronic, mechanical, photocopying, recording or otherwise, without the prior permission of the Publishers.

Bligh's Log © Crown Copyright 1981

Published by kind permission of the Controller of Her Majesty's Stationery Office

Illustrations by Roy Williams

ISBN 0 86134 032 9

Published in 1981 by Pageminster Press
Guildford, Surrey, England
in association with
Argot Press, Melbourne, Australia
and
Mitchell Beazley Ltd., 14–15 Manette Street, London, England.

Printed by Unwin Brothers Ltd, Woking, Surrey, England
Bound by Kemp Hall Bindery, Oxford, England

Foreword

The creak of flexing timbers vied with the soft moan of the wind in the taut rigging...water sloshed aimlessly below, a restless counterpoint to the grunts of sleeping men. The atmosphere was humid, rank, bitter-sweet with the scent of hibiscus. Gleaming beads of condensation ran down the freshly varnished

woodwork. An oppressive unease embraced the drifting vessel. But then...a footstep, a glint of metal...and the sleeping ship wakened abruptly to horror as her captain was hauled violently from his bed.

This was Bligh's first intimation of the mutiny that was to capture the imagination of scholar and layman alike over the ensuing 200 years. Indeed, several thousand books, articles and pamphlets, and three motion pictures, bear witness to the continuing fascination with the events of that fateful day.

Born in 1754, son of a Plymouth customs chief, William Bligh had joined the navy at 15. After five years as a midshipman, he had proved himself sufficiently gifted as a navigator and cartographer to attract the attention of James Cook, who invited him to sail on the *Resolution*, as Master — the most important position, from the ship-handling point of view. His subsequent acquaintance with the renowned naturalist Joseph Banks, a man of great influence, added further strength to Bligh's undoubted qualifications for command of the *Bounty*.

Built on the north-east coast of England by Wellbank, Sharp and Brown as a small (87-ft) three-masted, bluff-bowed trading vessel, *Bounty* (originally named

Bethia) was acquired by the Admiralty on the specific instructions of George III. She was completely refitted and rerigged at Deptford Yard, at a cost of £4,456 — against an original cost of £1,950 for the basic ship. The whole of her 'tween-decks was ripped out; and where the great cabin and officers' quarters should have been, a greenhouse was created. Designed to house about 1,000 bread-fruit plant saplings, it took up a third of the ship's overall length; and the resultant cramped conditions of the *Bounty*'s 46 officers and men were undoubtedly a contributory factor in the eventual mutiny.

On 23rd December 1787, *Bounty* set out from Spithead on her mission, which was to collect bread-fruit plants from Tahiti and convey them to the British West Indies, for transplantation. She reached Cape Horn in the atrocious conditions of mid-winter, her departure from England having been delayed considerably for various reasons.

Bligh had begun to realize on the voyage out that a number of his executives left much to be desired. The surgeon, James Huggan, was permanently drunk; John Fryer, the Master, had been insubordinate. The carpenter, Purcell, had proved himself a barrack-room lawyer, and many of the midshipmen were either too inexperienced or too lazy to be entrusted with much responsibility. And the ordinary seamen pressed from the taverns and brothels of southern England, while manageable enough at present, were a sure source of dissent should the strict shipboard discipline be at all relaxed.

The *Bounty*'s captain was not, however, the tyrant portrayed by the Hollywood film-makers. He publicly thanked his crew for their efforts in attempting to round the Horn (unaware that they had actually rounded Cape Horn on three occasions before being beaten back, he had finally turned about for the Cape of Good Hope); and he took every precaution, by shortening watch periods and providing warm, dry clothing and airing below decks, to ensure the healthiest conditions possible under prevailing conditions.

Because he was still only rated Lieutenant on leaving England, Bligh had been unable to bring with him officially appointed junior lieutenants. He therefore promoted Fletcher Christian, Master's mate, to acting lieutenant so that he could take third watch and act as executive second-in-command. They had sailed together twice before — in Duncan Campbell's *Britannia*, to the West Indies — and so must have been well acquainted with each other's strengths and weaknesses of character. If there is one criticism that can be fairly levelled at Bligh, it is that he did not suffer fools gladly. His very short temper led him frequently to critize; he even abused his officers in front of their subordinates, which was hardly conducive to a stable chain of command.

On reaching the Cape of Good Hope, they put in for provisions, rest and restoration of the ship, staying for 38 days. Making their way across the Southern Indian Ocean without touching Australia, they continued to Tasmania, where Bligh had formerly stopped with Cook to replenish supplies of food and water. From here, it was but a short run with the prevailing winds up to Tahiti.

Imagine, if you can, rising from an azure-blue sea, sheer pinnacles of rock, densely forested with magnificent skies behind, swathed in a gossamer haze of water droplets reflecting the brilliant sun. Here indeed was a new Eden for these weary men in their tiny vessel!

The Polynesians, whose small islands were divided into a number of kingdoms, traditionally greeted the white man in splendour and ceremony. Their own ruling families were kept apart from the rest of the population; and the royal skin, particularly that of women, was kept as light as possible. Thus, when a shipload of pale-skinned Europeans arrived, the native population believed it to be a visitation from another royal family. Their generosity would allow them to spare no  effort to provide everything the visitors might need, even to the point of starving themselves to ensure that sumptuous banquets could be offered throughout the guests' sojourn. Because their religion did not permit them aboard the canoes, the young women used to swim out to the ships — and in so doing, dissolved their beautifully made tapa-bark robes, to the gratified astonishment of men who had not seen a woman for well over a year.

Because the bread-fruit saplings were not yet ready for transplanting, the *Bounty's* officers and men remained for six months on that earthly paradise. During this period, instead of sending the ship on exploratory voyages, Bligh indulged his crew by allowing them generous shore-leave, which encouraged the rapid establishment of close friendships between the men and the native population. Bligh himself remained aloof on board, noting down what he had observed of the relationships, habits and manners of the islanders, and sketching their flora and fauna.

His dissatisfaction with the executive officers increased throughout their stay at Tahiti. Spare sets of sails, carelessly stored, were found mildewed and rotting; and important components went missing from the ship, as nails of copper and iron became the staple currency in the bartering for favours from the native women. Venereal disease (introduced by the island's first European visitors) was soon rife among the crew. Fletcher Christian earned Bligh's angry contempt by wenching openly and subsequently involving himself with one of the king's daughters; behaviour that may well have occasioned the virulent quarrels that occurred after the ship had left Tahiti.

Three deserters were brought back only after the natives of an outlying island were pressurized by Bligh into assisting in their recovery; *Bounty* barely escaped serious grounding after her anchor cable was cut, allegedly by a native who wished his new friends to remain on the island. Bligh's temper must have been badly strained: he must leave, and endeavour to restore discipline to his ragged band.

After a stay of 27 weeks, *Bounty* left Tahiti fully reprovisioned and sailed west towards the Friendly Islands. But it soon became apparent that the men were unwilling to shake down to the rigours of life on board. Squabbles flared over trivialities. Coconuts, collected in their hundreds at Tahiti, had been piled along the deck rails for future use as provisions. Small hogs, Tahiti's principal source of meat, had also been brought on board. Bligh's requisitioning of these private hoards for the common good caused much resentment, not least on the part of Christian. The two had an altercation on deck early one morning: Bligh noticed the lower height of one of the coconut piles

and rounded on Christian, accusing him of taking some for himself. The ensuing row ended with Christian sulking in his cabin. By nightfall, Bligh was typically ready to forget the incident and invited Christian to join him for supper; but the latter, still smarting, refused. It was the first public indication of a hostility of any depth.

In his distraught state, Christian sought aid from others aboard in purloining timber and other materials to make a small raft, with the intention of slipping over the side while they were still close to the Friendly Islands. But midshipman George Stewart implied that the men were "ripe for anything": surely it would better to return to England with Bligh in irons than to risk death from sharks or natives? Stewart's words raced through Christian's mind, feeding on his resentment, throughout that muggy night. They were just off the island of Tofua, and some of the men were trying to catch a shark that was basking alongside. A distant erupting volcano bathed the ocean in a warm glow. The midshipmen of the watch, Hayward and Hallett, were asleep on deck. John Fryer, before retiring to his cabin opposite Bligh's, had inexcusably passed the keys of the arms chest to the armourer — so that the shark-hunters could obtain a musket, if needed, without disturbing Fryer himself.

A perfect set of circumstances: the arms-chest keys insecure, the senior members of the watch asleep and a dissenting crew, half of whom longed to return to the delights of Tahiti... The resolution was quickly made and the ship was seized.

Bligh was dragged up on deck in his night-shirt. It was resolved to put him into the small cutter; but on launching, it was seen to have rotted. This fact would not have deterred the hard-liners; but it soon became clear that more men wanted to go with Bligh than wanted to remain, and with the prospect of a possible counter-action against Christian and his party, it became essential for the mutineers to rid themselves of the majority of the loyal crew-members. Accordingly, the launch — a 23-ft open boat — was put into the water and 19 men were forced into it. Then it was cast adrift on the uncharted seas, with the minimum of provisions: 28 gallons of water, 150 lb ship's biscuit, 20 lb pork, five gallons of rum, three bottles of wine, some coconuts and bread-fruit. No arms were provided, although four cutlasses were grudgingly thrown down at the last minute, in exchange for a watch, as the two vessels drifted apart. The last thing Bligh heard was the mutineers' cry: "Huzza for Otaheite!" He had tried in every way to remonstrate with his second-in-command ("You have dangled my children on your knee...") but the die was cast; and Christian's last words to him as he descended into the launch had been: "That is it, Captain Bligh, I am in Hell."

The 4,000-mile voyage in the open boat, with barely six inches of clearance between the top of the boat's side and the water when calm, is one of the truly heroic deeds of British naval history. Of the 19 men Bligh took with him, only one died on the voyage — and he (John Norton, quartermaster) was killed by natives on Tofua the following day.

Despite their meagre provision for the daunting journey, and notwithstanding bitter quarrels (between Purcell, Fryer and Bligh) along the route, they reached the Dutch settlement of Timor in 41 days. There they received much help from the willing Governor before going on to join a ship to take them back to England. Owing to their generally weakened state, however, they were particularly susceptible to malaria and the other tropical diseases then rife in the Dutch East Indies, and despite the earnest efforts of Bligh and his hosts, six of the men died. Those remaining were obliged to make their way back to England on separate vessels, one of which foundered.

On his return, Bligh was court-martialled for the loss of his ship but was honourably acquitted. He was supplied with a second ship, the *Providence*, to repeat his ill-fated voyage in company with a small tender, *The Assistant*; and in 1793 he returned again to England, having accomplished all he had set out to achieve, including confirmation of his discovery, while in the open boat, of the principal section of the 47 Fiji Isles. He went on to greater heights, including Nelson's publicly expressed gratitude for his assistance in the action at Copenhagen. His involvement in the quelling of the great mutinies of 1797 is well recorded; while his subsequent appointment as Governor-General of New South Wales did much to further British colonial rule. Bligh died a Rear Admiral of the Blue, in 1817, and was buried in Lambeth Churchyard, on the south bank of the Thames.

As for the mutineers: the *Pandora* was sent in search of them under the command of Captain Edward Edwards, a less imaginative man than Bligh and a stronger disciplinarian; but the core of the band had left with Christian on the *Bounty*, after an abortive attempt to establish a colony on an outlying island of the Austral Group, Tubuai.

There were some aboard *Bounty* who had soon come to regret their actions. Christian had therefore returned to Tahiti to put them ashore, and had then set sail by night, with eight mutineer accomplices and 18 native men, women and a child, to find an uninhabited island for their future home.

Captain Edwards took back the repentant mutineers left on Tahiti, but never tracked down Fletcher and his team. *Pandora* herself was wrecked, on the Great Barrier Reef; and for her survivors, who included ten of the mutineers, it was then an open-boat voyage to the Dutch East Indies and thence by merchant vessel back to England. The returning mutineers stood trial: four were acquitted, two pardoned and three hanged for their crimes. One, Muspratt, got off on a technicality.

Christian, whether by luck or by design, arrived eventually at Pitcairn Island, a great pillar of rock rising sheer out of the ocean off the west coast of South America. Here he attempted to establish a colony; but old habits die hard, and within a couple of years all but one of his fellow mutineers had been murdered, by colleagues or by natives. The remaining man, John Adams (known aboard *Bounty* as Alexander Smith), then installed himself as patriarch of the Pitcairn community, which continued to grow — and remained undiscovered by the outside world until 1808, when an American sealing captain, Mayhew Folger, called at the island for water. By that time, there was a thriving colony of mixed-race children; but only one white mutineer.

In view of the Admiralty's involvement in the war in Europe, nothing was done to bring Adams back to justice. In 1818 and 1828, passing expeditions called at Pitcairn and questioned him; but he told conflicting stories of the early days of the colony, and of the fate of Fletcher Christian. Adams died shortly after the visit from the second expedition; but in 1831, in his book *The Mutiny and Piratical Seizure of HMS Bounty*, the then second secretary to the Admiralty, Sir John Barrow, recalled that midshipman Peter Heywood (who went to Tahiti with Christian but was brought back on *Pandora* and survived her wrecking) had been quoted as saying he believed he had seen Christian in the early 1800s — in Plymouth, England.

It is in the many twists and turns, in the intriguing blend of improbable fact and reasonable surmise, that the saga of the *Bounty* and her crew lives on. The following pages — a facsimile portion of the official Admiralty copy of the Log, signed by Bligh — contain the full day-to-day account of the mutiny itself and the danger and hardships of the open-boat voyage that followed. Now you can learn from Bligh's own words the facts of the story that began so dramatically on 28th April 1789.

Stephen Walters

The Bounty's Crew

Name	Rank	Age	Place of birth (where known)
A William Bligh	Lieutenant	33	St. Tudy, Cornwall
A John Fryer	Master	33	Wells, Norfolk
A William Cole	Boatswain		
A William Peckover	Gunner		
A William Purcell	Carpenter		
D Thomas Huggan	Surgeon		
A Thomas Ledward	Surgeon's Mate		
A William Elphinstone	Master's Mate	36	Edinburgh
GB Fletcher Christian	Master's Mate	22	Cockermouth, Cumberland
A John Hallet	Midshipman	15	London
BI Peter Heywood	Midshipman	15	Douglas, Isle of Man
A Thomas Hayward	Midshipman	20	Hackney, London
BG Edward Young	Midshipman	21	St. Kitts, West Indies
BF George Stewart	Midshipman	21	Orkney
A Robert Tinkler	Midshipman	17	East Anglia
A John Norton	Quarter master	34	Liverpool
A Peter Linkletter	Quarter master	30	Shetland
A George Simpson	Quarter master's Mate	27	Kendal, Westmorland
BFI James Morrison	Boatswain's Mate	27	London
BG John Mills	Gunner's Mate	39	Aberdeen, Scotland
CF Charles Norman	Carpenter's Mate	24	Portsmouth, Hampshire
CF Thomas McIntosh		25	North Shields, Tyne and Wear
A Lawrence Lebogue	Sailmaker	40	
CF Joseph Coleman	Armourer	36	Guildford, Surrey
BH Charles Churchill	Corporal	25	Manchester
BF Henry Hillbrandt	Cooper	24	Hanover, Germany
BF William Muspratt	Steward	27	Maidenhead, Berkshire
A John Samuel	Clerk	26	Edinburgh
A Thomas Hall	Cook	38	Durham
A John Smith	Captain's Servant	38	Stirling, Scotland
A Robert Lamb	Butcher	21	London
BF Richard Skinner	Able Seaman	22	Tunbridge Wells
BG Alexander Smith		20	London
BFJ Thomas Burkitt		25	Bath
BFJ John Millward		21	Plymouth
BG John Williams		26	Stepney, London
BF John Sumner		22	Liverpool
BH Matthew Thompson		37	Isle of Wight
E James Valentine		28	Montrose, Scotland
BF Michael Byrne		26	Kilkenny, Ireland
BG William McCoy		23	
BG Mathew Quintal		21	
BH Isaac Martin		30	Philadelphia, U.S.A.
BFJ Thomas Ellison		19	Deptford, London
A David Nelson	Gardener		
BG William Brown	Gardener's Assistant	25	

KEY

A = Open boat
B = Mutineer
C = Kept against will
D = Died at Tahiti (natural causes)
E = Died before Tahiti (natural causes)

F = Returned on *Pandora*
G = Went to Pitcairn
H = Killed by natives
I = Pardoned
J = Hanged

The Log
in
Facsimile

The following pages, here reproduced in facsimile, form a portion of the Admiralty copy of Bligh's Log, reference ADM 55/151. The original is housed at the Public Record Office, Kew.

Remarks. Tuesday 28th April 1789 at Sea.

Light Winds and Cloudy Wr — Wind NE — E and E SE.

I kept near the Ogodoo untill 5 OClock this afternoon in hopes to have had some Cannoes off but I saw none. I therefore directed my Course to the West and went to the Southward of Tofoa. — Mr Fryer the Master had the first Watch, Mr Peckover the Gunner the Middle, and Mr Christian one of the Mates the Morning Watch — This was the tour of duty for the Night. —

I just before Sun rise Mr Christian. Mate, Chas Churchill Ships Corporal, John Mills Gunners Mate and Thomas Burkitt, Seaman — came into my Cabbin while I was asleep and seizing me tyed my hands with a Cord behind my back and threatned me with instant death if I spoke or made the least noise — I however called so loud as to alarm every one, but the Officers found themselves secured by Centinels at their Doors. — There were four Men in my Cabbin and three outside viz. Alexr Smith. Jno Sumner and Matw Quintal. — Mr Christian had a Cutlass in his hand, the others had Musquets and Bayonets. — I was forced on Deck in my Shirt, suffering great pain from the Violence with which they had tied my hands — I demanded the reason for such a violent act: but I received no Answer but threats of instant death if I did not hold my tongue. — Mr Hayward & Hallett were in Mr Christians Watch, but had no Idea that any thing was doing untill they were all armed. — The Arms were all Secured so that no one could get near them for Centinels. — Mr Elphinstone the Mate was secured to his Birth. — Mr Nelson Botanist. Mr Peckover Gunner. Mr Ledward Surgeon & the Master were confined to their Cabbins, as also Mr Jno Samuel, (Clerk) but who from finesse got leave to come upon Deck. — The Fore Hatchway was guarded by Centinels, the Boatswain and Carpenter were however allowed to come on Deck where they saw me standing abaft the Mizen Mast with my hands tied behind my back, under a Guard with Christian at their Head. —

The Boatswain was now ordered to hoist the Boat out, with a threat if he did not do it instantly to take care of himself. —

Mr Hayward and Hallett. Midshipmen, and Mr Samuel were now ordered into the Boat upon which I assumed my authority and demanded the Cause of such an Order, at the same time endeavouring to bring some one to a sense of his duty, but it was to no effect. "Hold your tongue Sir or you are dead this Instant" was constantly repeated to me. —

The Master by this time had sent to be allowed to come on Deck and was permitted, and as soon was Ordered back to his Cabbin again, when he returned. —

I continued to indeavor to change the Tide of affairs, when Christian changed the Cuttlass he had in his hand for a Bayonet that was brought to him, and holding me with a Strong Grip by the cord that tied my hands, he continued to threaten me with instant death if I did not be quiet. — The Villains round me had their pieces Cocked & Bayonets fixed, and particular People were now Called upon to go in the Boat, and were hurried over the side, — With these people I concluded of course I was to be set a drift. I therefore in making another effort to bring about a Change expressed myself in such a Manner as to be saluted with "Blow his Brains out". —

The Boatswain and Seamen who were to go in the Boat, collected twine, canvas, lines Sails, Cordage an eight and twenty Gallon Cask of Water, and the Carpenter got his Tool Chest. — Mr Samuel got 150 lbs Bread with a Small quantity of Rum and Wine — He also got a Quadrant and Compass into the Boat, but forbid on Pain of death of touching any Map whatever. Ephemeris Book of Astronomical

Observations - Sextants - Time Keeper or any of my Surveys or drawings. —

The Mutineers were now hurrying every one into the Boat, and the most of them being in, Christian directed a Dram to be served to each of his Crew. — I was now exceedingly fatigued, and unhappily saw I could do nothing to effect the Recovery of the Ship - every endeavor was threatened with death, and the following People were now in the Boat. —

John Fryer	Master
Thos. Denmn. Ledward	Surgeon
David Nelson	Botanist
Willm. Peckover	Gunner
Willm. Cole	Boatswain
Willm. Purcell	Carpenter
Willm. Elphinstone	Masters Mate
Thos. Hayward	Midn
John Hallett	Midn
John Norton	Qur Master
Peter Linkletter	Qur Master
Sawe. Lebogue	Sail Maker
John Smith	Ab
Thos. Hall	Ab
Geo: Simpson	Qur Masters Mate
Robt. Tinkler	Ab
Robt. Lamb	Ab
John Samuel	Clerk

There remained on board as Pirates and under Arms

Fletcher Christian	Masters Mate
Peter Heywood	Midn
George Stewart	Midn
Edwd. Young	Midn

Charles	Churchill	Ships Corporal
John	Mills	Gunners Mate
James	Morrison	Boatsⁿˢ Mate
Thoˢ	Burkett	Ab
Mathew	Quintal	Ab
John	Sumner	Ab
John	Millward	Ab
Willᵐ	Mickoy	Ab
Henⁱ	Hilbrant	Ab
Willᵐ	Muspratt	Ab
Alexʳ	Smith	Ab
John	Williams	Ab
Thoˢ	Ellison	Ab
Isaac	Martin	Ab
Richᵈ	Skinner	Ab
Mathew	Thompson	Ab
Willᵐ	Brown	Botanists Assistant
Michˡ	Byrne	Ab
Joseph	Coleman	Armourer
Chaˢ	Norman	Carpenters Mate
Thoˢ	McIntosh	Dᵒˢ Crew

—— In all 25 Hands and the most able

Men on board the Ship. ——

This is breifly the Statement of the Case. — The Officers were called and forced into the Boat. while I was under a Guard abaft the Mizen Mast, Christian holding me by the Bandage that secured my hands with one hand, and a Baronet in the other. The Men under Arms round me had their Pieces cocked which so enraged me against those ungratefull Wretches that

I dared them to fire and they uncocked them. —

Isaac Martin one of the Guard I saw I had brought to a sense of his duty, and as he fed me with Shaddock, (my lips being so parched in endeavoring to bring about a Change in my Situation,) we explained to each other by our Eyes reciprocally our Wishes: This was however Observed, and Martin was instantly removed from me whose inclination then was to leave the Ship, but for a threat of instant death if he did not return out of the Boat. —

The Armourer Joseph Coleman and the two Carpenters McIntosh and Norman were kept Contrary to their inclination, and they begged of me After I was veered astern in the Boat to remember that they declared they had no hand in the transaction. Michl: Byrne the Fidler who is half blind I am told had no knowledge of what was done and Wanted to leave the Ship. —

It is of no moment for me to recount my endeavors to rally and bring to a sense of their duty the Offenders - all I could do was by Speaking to every one in general, for no one was suffered to come near me, I did my duty as far as it was possible to save the Ship, and they knew me too Well to put much in my power and therefore bound me very securely,

To Mr Samuel I am indebted for Securing to me my Journals and Commission with some Material Ships Papers - Without these I had nothing to Certify what I had done, and my honor and Character would have been in the power of Calumny without a proper document to have defended it. — All this he did with great resolution being guarded and Strictly Watched. — He attempted to save the Time Keeper and a Box with all my Surveys, Drawings and remarks for 15 years past which were numerous. Among which were my general Surveys of the West Coast of America, East Coast of Asia, the Sandwich and Friendly Islands. When he was hurried away with "damn Your Eyes you are well off to get what you have"

353

The Masters Cabbin was opposite to mine, he saw them in my Cabbin for our Eyes met each other through his Door Window—He had a pair of ships Pistols loaded and ammunition in his Cabbin—A firm resolution might have made a good Use of them.—These Pistols I had ordered for the Use of the Officer of the Watch since the 24th of January in case of desertion in the Night and they were at first kept in the Binnacle, but upon consideration that they might be stolen from thence they were ever after kept in the Masters Cabbin—After he had sent twice or thrice to Christian to be allowed to come on Deck he was at last permitted and his question then was will you let me remain in the Ship?—No.—Have you any objection Captn Bligh?—I whispered to him knock him down—Martin is good.—for this was just before Martin was removed from me. Christian however pulled me back, and the Master went away with Orders to go again to his Cabbin. and I saw no more of him untill he was put into the Boat.—He afterwards told me on my questioning him that he could find no Body to act with, that by staying in the Ship he hoped to have retaken her, and that as to the Pistols he was so flurried and surprized that he did not recollect he had them.—His Brother said on my enquiring how the Keys of the Arm Chest came out of his Cabbin, that Richard Skinner who attended on him had taken them away which was certainly the case.

As for the Officers whose Cabbins were in the Cockpitt, there was no relief for them—they endeavored to come to my Assistance; but were not allowed to put their heads above the Hatchway.—

The Boatswain and Carpenter were fully at liberty—the former was employed on pain of death to hoist the Boats out, but the latter

I saw acting the part of an Idler with an impudent and ill looking countenance which led me to believe he was one of the Mutineers, untile he was among the rest Ordered to leave the Ship, for it appeared to me to be a doubt with Christian at first, whether he should keep the Carpenter or his Mates, but knowing the former to be a troublesome fellow he determined on the latter. — The Carpenter was then Ordered into the Boat, upon which he got his Tool Chest with little difficulty over the Side. —

Much altercation took place among the Mutinous Crew during the whole business — some Swore "I'll be damned if he does not get home if he gets any thing with him (meaning me) — Others when the Carpenters Chest was carrying away" Damn my Eyes he will have a Vessel built in a Month; while others laughed at the Situation of the Boat being very deep. and not room for those that were in her. — As for Christian he seemed to be pleadding instant destruction on himself and every one, for of all diavolical looking Men he exceeded every possible description. —

I asked for Arms but they laughed at me and said I was well acquainted where I was going and therefore did not want them. Four Cutlasses were however thrown into the Boat. after She was veered astern. —

When the Officers and Men were put into the Boat (with whom I was suffered to have no communication) they only then Waited for me, and the Ships Corporal informed Christian of it, who then told me Come Captr Bligh your Officers and Men are now in the Boat. and you must go with them, If you attempt to make the least resistance you will instantly be put to death and forcing me before him, holding by the Cord that frapped my hands behind my back and a Bayonet in his other, with a Tribe of Armed Ruffians about me I was forced over the Side where they untied my hands, and being in the Boat we were veered astern by a Rope. — A few pieces of Pork were now thrown into us and some Cloaths, and after having undergone a great deal of redicule we were at last cast adrift in the open Ocean. — Having little or no wind we rowed pretty fast towards Tofoa which bore N E about 10 leagues. and while the Ship was in sight she Steered to the WNW, but I consider that as a blind to me for when we came away, Huzza for Otaheite was frequently heard among the Mutineers. —

Christian the Captain of the Mutineers. is of a respectable Family in the North of England. — This was the third Voyage he had made with me, and as I found it necessary to keep my Ships Company at three Watches. I gave him an Order to keep the third, his abilities being thoroughly equal to the task, and by this means my Master and Gunner were not at Watch and Watch. —

Heywood is also of a respectable family in the North of England and a Young Man of Abilities as well as Christian. — These two were objects of my regard and attention and with much unwearied Zeal I instructed them for they realy promised as professional Men to be an honor to their Country. —

Young was a Person recommended to me by Sir George Young Captain in the Navy. He appeared to me to be an able and stout Seaman and therefore I took him, he however always proved a Worthless Wretch. —

Stewart was a Young Man of creditable Parents in the Orkneys, He was a Seaman and bore a good Character. —

Here we may observe to what a height the baseness of human Nature may arrive at, not only ingratitude in its blackest die, but eternal criminality against their Country and connections. —

I had scarce got a furlong on my way when I began

to reflect on the vicisitudes of human affairs; but in the midst of all I felt an inward happiness which prevented any depression of my Spirits, conscious of my own integrity and anxious solicitude for the good of the Service I was on. — I found my mind most wonderfully Supported, and began to conceive hopes notwithstanding so heavy a Calamity, to be able to recount to my King and Country my misfortune. —

What Mans situation could be so peculiarly flattering as mine twelve hours before? — I had a Ship in the most perfect order and well Stored with every necessary both for service and health, by early attention to those particulars I had acted against the power of Chance in case I could not get through Endeavor Streights as well as against any Accident that might befall me in them, and to add to this I had very successfully got my Plants in the most flourishing and fine order, so that upon the whole the Voyage was two thirds completed and the remaining part no Way doubtfull, — Every person in the most perfect health to establish which I had taken the greatest pains and bore a most anxious care the whole course of the Voyage. —

It is certainly true that no effect could take place without a Cause, but here it is equally certain that no cause could justify such an effect — It however may very naturally be asked what could be the reason for such a revolt, in Answer to which I can only conjecture that they have Idealy assured themselves of a more happy life among the Otaheiteans than they could possibly have in England, which joined to some Female connections has most likely been the leading cause of the whole business. —

The Women are handsome — mild in their Manners and conversation — possessed of great sensibility, and have sufficient delicacy to make them admired and beloved. — The Cheifs have acquired such a liking to our People that they have rather encouraged their stay among them than otherwise, and even made promises of large possessions.— Under these and many other attendant circumstances equally desireable it is therefore now not to be Wondered at, 'tho not possible to be foreseen, that a Set of Sailors led by Officers, and void of connections, or if they have any, not possessed of Natural feelings sufficient to Wish themselves never to be seperated from them, should be governed by such powerfull inducements.— but equal to this, what a temptation it is to such Wretches when they find it in their power however illegally it can be got at, to fix themselves in the Midst of plenty in the finest Island in the World where they need not labour, and where the alurements of disipation are more than equal to any thing that can be conceived.

Desertions have happened more or less from the Ships that have been at the Society Islands, but it ever has been in the Commanders power to make the Chiefs return their people — They therefore knew such a plan could never succeed, and perhaps suggested that never so small a Ship and so elligible an opportunity would offer to them again.—

The Secrecy of this Mutiny is beyond all Conception, and surprizing it is that out of thirteen of the party who were sent with me and lived always forward among the People, and the Messmates of Christian, Stewart, Heywood & Young, no one could discover some symptoms of bad intentions among them.— This Mutiny or design against the Ship has however been long planned if I with propriety may take the cutting of the Cable as a beginning on the 6th Feby for that act was certainly done by some of these People to strand the Ship, altho at that time I naturally thought it was done by the Indians, but who it now appears were certainly innocent. — With such deep laid plans of Villany and my mind free of any Suspicions it is not wonderful I have been got the better of. — But the possibility of such a Catastrophe, was ever the farthest from my thoughts. — Christian was to have dined with me and supped the preceeding Evening, but he desired to be excused as he found himself unwell, about which I was concerned rather than suspecting his integrity and honor. —

It now remained with me what was best to be done, and I determined that after getting a Supply of Bread fruit and Water at Tofoa to sail for Amsterdam and there risk a Solicitation to Paulehow to equip my Boat and grant a Supply so as to enable me to return towards Home. —

The exact quantity of Provisions I found they had got in the Boat was 150 lbs Bread 16 pieces of Pork, 6 Quarts of Rum. 6 Bottles of Wine with 28 Gall of Water and four Empty Breakers. —

Wm Bligh

Description of the Pirates

Fletcher Christian 24   age   Masters Mate — 5"9 High. — Blackish or very dark brown Complexion Dark Brown Hair. — Strong Made. A Star tatowed on his left Breast and tatowed on the backside His Knees stand a little out and he may be called a little Bow legged, He is subject to Violent perspiration, particularly in his hands so that he Soils any thing he handles. —

Geo: Stewart 23   Midshipman — 5"7. High. Good Complexion, Dark Hair Slender Made, Narrow chested and long Neck. A Star tatowed on the left Breast and One on the left Arm with a heart and darts. — Tatowed on the backside. — Small Face and black Eyes. —

Peter Heywood 17.   Midshipman — 5"7 — High Fair Complexion, light Brown Hair — well proportioned. — very much tatowed. & on the Right leg is tatowed the Legs of Man as the impression on that Coin is. — At this time he had not done growing and Speaks with the Manks or Isle of Man Accent. —

Edwᵈ Young 22   Midshipman 5"8 High. — Dark Complexion and rather a bad look, Dark brown Hair. Strong made, has lost several of his Fore teeth, and those that remain are rotten. — A Small mole on the left side of the throat and on the Right Arm is tatowed a Heart and Dart through it with E:Y underneath and the date of the Year 1788 or 1789. —

Chaᵈ: Churchill 30   Ships Corporal — 5"10. High. Fair Complexion, short light brown Hair. Top of the Head Bald. Strong Made. the Fore Finger of his left hand Crooked. and his hand shews the mark of a Severe Scald. — Tatowed on Several places of his Body, Legs and Arms. —

	Age	

Ja.^s Morrison — 28 — Boats.^{ns} Mate — 5 F. 8 In High. Sallow Complexion, Long Black Hair, Slender Made. has lost the use of the upper joint of the Fore finger of the Right hand. — Tatowed with a Star under his left Breast, and a Garter round his left Leg with the Motto of Honi soit qui mal.^y pense. and has been Wounded in One of his Arms with a Musquet Ball. —

John Mills — 40 — Gunners Mate. 5 F. 10 In. — Fair Complexion, Light Brown Hair Strong Made Raw Boned. — A Scar in his Right Arm pitt Occasioned by an Abcess. —

Jno Millward — 22 — Ab. — 5 F. 5 In High. Brown Complexion, Dark Hair, Strong Made, very much tatowed in different parts of the Body and under the pit of the Stomach with a Tàoomy or Breast plate of Otaheite. —

Mat.^w Thompson — 40 — Ab — 5 F. 8 In High — Very dark Complexion, Short black Hair. Slender Made. and has lost the joint of the Great Toe of his Right Foot and is tatowed in several places of his body. —

Willm Mickoy — 25 — Ab. — 5 F. 6 In. High. Fair Complexion, Light Brown Hair, Strong Made. A Scar where he has been Stabbed in the Belly, and a Small Scar under his Chin. is Tatowed in different parts of the Body. —

Mat.^w Quintal — 21 — Ab — 5 F. 5 In. High. Fair Complexion, Light Brown Hair, Strong made, Very much tatowed on the backside and Several other places. —

Jno Sumner — 24 — Ab — 5 F. 8 In. High Fair Complexion, Brown Hair, Slender Made, A Scar upon the left Cheek and tatowed in several places. —

Thos Burkitt — 26 — Ab — 5 F. 9 In High. Fair Complexion, very much pitted with the Small Pox. Brown Hair. Well made and very much tatowed. —

Isaac Martin — 30 — Ab. — 5 F. 11 In. High. Sallow Complexion short brown Hair, Raw Boned. tatowed with a Star on his left Breast. —

                  Age

Will.m Muspratt. 30 Ab — 5.6 High.d Dark Complexion, Brown Hair, Slender Made — A very Strong Black Beard. with Scars under his Chin, is tatowed on several places of his Body

Hen.y Hilbrant 25 Ab — 5..7 High Fair Complexion — Sandy Hair Strong made. his left Arm shorter than the other having been broke is a Hanoverian Born & speaks bad English is tatowed in several places. —

Alex.r Smith. 22 Ab — 5..5 High Brown Complexion Brown Hair, Strong Made. very much pitted with the Small Pox. and very much tatowed on his Body, Legs, Arms, and Feet. and has a Scar on his Right Foot. where he has been cut with a Wood Axe. —

Jn.o Williams. 25 Ab — 5..5 High Dark Complexion Black Hair, Slender Made, has a Scar on the back part of his Head is tatowed — A Native of Guernsey & Speaks French —

Rich.d Skinner 22 Ab. — 5..8 High, Very well made. has Scars on both Ankles and on his Right shin is very much tatowed and by Trade a Hair Dresser —

Mich.l Byrn. 28 Ab — 5..6 High Fair Complexion, short fair Hair Slender Made, is almost Blind and has the marks of an Issue on the back of his Neck. — Plays the Violin. —

Tho.s Ellison :17 Ab — 5..3 High Fair Complexion. Dark Hair, Strong Made has got his Name Tatowed on his Right Arm and dated Oct.r 25.th 1788 —

Will.m Brown 27 Botanists Assistant. 5..8 High Fair Complexion, Dark Brown Hair. Slender Made a Remarkable Scar on One of his Cheeks which contracts the Eye lid & runs down to his throat occasioned by the Kings Evil — is tatowed —

	Age.		F I	

Jos.^h Coleman 40 Armourer — 5..6 High. Fair Complexion, Grey Hair, Strong Made A Heart tattowed on One of his Arms.. —

Thos Mc Intosh 20 Carpenters Crew — 5..6 High. Fair Complexion, Light brown Hair. Slender Made. is pitted with the Small Pox. is tattowed

Chas Norman 26 Carpenter Mate — 5..9 High. Fair Complexion Light brown Hair. Slender Made is pitted with the Small Pox; has a remarkable Motion with his Head and Eyes —

<u>Rem.^s in the Bounty's Launch. Wednesday 29th April 1789 at Tofoa</u>

Happily the Afternoon kept Calm untill about 4 O'Clock, when we were so far to Windward that with a Moderate Easterly breeze which sprung up we were able to sail — it was nevertheless dark when we got under Tofoa where I expected to land, but the Shore proved to be so steep and Rocky that I was obliged to give up all thoughts of it and keep the Boat under the Island with two Oars, for there was no landing   Having fixed on this mode of proceeding for the Night. I served to every person two Gills of Grog, and each took his rest in proportion as they reflected on their unhappy Situation

In the Morning at dawn of day we set off along shore in search of landing, and about 10 OClock we discovered a Stoney Cove at the NW part of the Island where I dropt the Grapnel within 20 Yards of the Rocks. — A great deal of Surf run on the Shore, but as I determined to encrease our Original Stock of provisions rather than diminish it, I sent out Mr Samuel and some others who Climbed the Cliff to get into the Country to search for Supplies. — The rest of us remained at the Cove after discovering no way to get into the Country but that by which Mr Samuel had proceeded. — I became happy to find the spirits and life of my people were raised, and that our miserable Situation may be forever known to the World. I made an Observation of the Latitude which determines this Cove to lie in 19..41 S° on the NW side of Tofoa. — N° Westermost of the Friendly Islands — The whole Coast we have seen is an entire precipice. — Towards Noon Mr Samuel returned with a few Quarts of Water which he had found in the holes, of thethat he had met with no Spring or any prospect of our Wants being relieved in that particular, and that he had only seen signs of the Island being inhabited. As it was impossible to say how much we might be in Want. I only issued a Morsel of Bread & a Glass of Wine to each person for Dinner. —

Fair W^r. but the Wind blew so violently from the E S E that I could not venture to Sea — our detention therefore made it absolutely necessary to see what we could do more for our support, for I determined if possible to keep my first Stock entire. I therefore Weighed and rowed along shore to the South^d to see what was to be got, and at last discovered some Cocoa Nutt Trees but they were on the Tops of high precipices and the Surf made it dangerous land= ing — both One and the other we however got the better of. some with much difficulty and Risk climbed the Clifts and got about 20 Cocoa Nutts. and the others Slung them to Ropes in the surf by which we hauled them into the Boat. — This was all could be done here, and as I found no place so elligble as the One we left to spend the Night at. I returned to the Cove, and having served a Cocoa Nutt to each person we went to rest again in the Boat. —

At dawn of day I attempted to get to Sea, but the Wind and Weather proved so bad. that I was glad to get back to my former Station, where after issuing a Morsel of Bread. and a Spoonfull of Rum to each person, we landed and I went off with Mr Nelson, Mr Samuel and some others into the Country, having hauled ourselves up the precipice by long Vines which were fixed there by the Natives for that purpose, this being the only way into the Cove. —

We found a few deserted Hutts and a small Plantain Walk but little taken care of. from which we could only collect three Small bunches of Plantains. — After pasing this place We fell in with a deep Gulley that led towards the Mountains near the Vulcano, and as I conceived that in the Rainy Season very great torrents of Water must pass through it. — we hoped to find sufficient for our Use remaining in some holes of the Rocks — After searching some time the whole that could be got were only Nine Gallons in the course of the Day. — We were advanced within two miles of the foot of the highest land in the Island on which is a Vulcano that is almost constantly burning. — the Country near it was all covered with lava and had a horrible appearance, and as we had not been fortunate in our discoveries and saw but little to alleviate our distresses, We filled our Cocoa Nutt shells with What Water we could find and returned exceedingly fatigued and faint. — When I came to where we were to descend into the Cove I found the Precipice which I had got up with little trouble to give me a difficult task to get down, for I was siezed with such a dizziness in my head that I thought it scarce possible to effect it, however by the asistance of Mr Nelson and others they at last got me down in a weak condition. — Being all returned by Noon I gave about an Oz of Pork and two Plantains to each person with about a half Glass of Wine, and I observed again the Latd of this place to be 19..41 South. — The People who remained by the Boat I directed to look out for Fish or what they could pick up about the Rocks, but nothing eatable could be found, so that upon the whole we considered ourselves upon as miserable a Spot of land as could well be found. —

I could not say positively from what former knowledge I had of this Island whether it was inhabited or not; but I knew it was not considered equal to the other of the Friendly Islands. and I was not certain but that the Natives only resorted to it at particular times I was therefore very Anxious to discover this Point, for in case there were only a few here and those could give us but very Moderate Supplies I thought of making some improvement on my Boat on the Spot. rather than risk going among Multitudes where perhaps I might lose every thing. — A party therefore who found themselves sufficiently strong I determined should go another Route as soon as the Sun became lower and they chearfully undertook it. — At the head of the Cove was a Cave about 150 Yards from the Water side and Across the Stony Beach it was about 100 Yards, with only the one way into the Cove that I have described. The situation was thus far good with respect to our not being Surprized, and I determined to remain on shore all the Night with a part of my people that the others might have more room to rest in the Boat with the Master, who I gave directions to lay at a Grapnel and be Watchfull in case we should be attacked Thus far my determinations to Noon when each of us endeavored to get a Couple of Hours Sleep. —

Stormy Wr with Rain in the Night Wind at E S E and S E. —

About 2 Oclock this afternoon, the Party set out in search of Water, but after suffering much Fatigue they returned in the Evening without any kind of Success. — I ordered one Plantain for each person to be boiled and having supped on this scanty Allowance with a Gill of Grog and fixed the Watches for the Night those whose turn it was laid down to sleep in the Cave before which we kept up a good Fire. — We were notwithstanding troubled with many Flys & Musquitoes. —

At dawn of day the Party set out again on a different route to see what they could get, in the course of which they again suffered greatly for want of Water — They however met with two Men a Woman and a Child, the Men came with them to the Cove and brought two Cocoa Nutt Shells of Water. — I immediatly made friends with these People and sent them away for Breadfruit, Plantains, and a few Cocoa Nutt Shells of Water. — Soon after other Natives came to us and by Noon I had 30 of them about me trading with the above Articles which relieved us from hunger and thirst, but I could only afford 1 oz of Pork and a quarter of a Bread fruit pr Man for dinner with a couple of Gills of Water; for I was fixed in not using any Bread or Water out of the Boat. — No particular theif was yet amongst us, the Natives were notwithstanding tractable and behaved honestly, giving their Articles for a few Buttons and Beads. — The Party who had been out informed me of having discovered several neat Plantations, so that it became no longer a doubt of there being fixed inhabititants on the Island, and I therefore determined to get what I could and Sail the first Moment the Wind and Weather would allow me to put to Sea. —

Rem^s in the Bountys Launch Saturday 2nd May 1789 at Tofoa. —

Stormy W^r Wind ESE

It had hitherto been a weighty consideration with me how I was to account to the Natives for the loss of my Ship. I knew they had too much good sense to be amused with a story that the Ship was to join me, when they all knew from the Hills she was not in sight it therefore rested whether I was to tell the real fact, or that the Ship had overset and sunk and that only us were Saved. — The latter appeared to me the most proper and advantageous to us, and I accordingly told every one that we were all to agree in one story. — As I expected, enquiries were made after the Ship and they seemed readily satisfyed with our Account, but there did not appear the least mark of Joy or sorrow in their Faces, altho' I fancied I discovered some signs of surprize — Some or other were coming and going the whole Afternoon, and we got enough Breadfruit, Plantains and Cocoa Nutts for to morrow, but Water they only brought us about 5 pints. — A Cannoe also came in with four Men and brought a few Breadfruit, those I bought also for Buttons and Beads. Nails were much enquired after but I would not suffer one to be shown, as I wanted them for the use of the Boat. —

Towards Evening I saw with peculiar pleasure that we had encreased our Stock of Provisions, and that at Sun down the Natives left us in quiet possession of the Cove. — I thought this a good Sign and made no doubt that they would come again with a larger proportion of Food and Water with which I hoped to sail without any farther delay, and that then In case in my attempt to get to Amsterdam I should be blown away from the Islands altogether, I should have a larger quantity of provisions to support me against so heavy a Calamity. —

At Night I served ¼ of a Breadfruit and a Cocoa Nutt to each person for Supper and having made a good fire all those but the Watch went to sleep. —

At day break I was happy to find every ones Spirits a little revived and saw not those anxious looks towards me for what was best to be done, as they have been since we left the Ship, but every countenance appeared to have a degree of Chearfullness and manfully looked Forward to do their best. — As I now only doubted of Water being brought to me a party set off among the Gullies in the Mountains with Empty Shells to see what they could get, and in their absence the Natives came about us as I expected and more numerous. also two Cannoes came in from round the North side of the Island in One of which was an elderly Chief called Macca-ackavou. — soon after a good looking Chief came down with some of our Party who were out forraging, called Eegijeefou or perhaps more properly Eefou, Eegij or Eghee signifying a Chief — To both these Men I made a present of an Old Shirt and a Knife, and I soon found they either saw me or had heard of my being at Anamoka. They also knew I had been with Captn. Cook who they enquired after and also Captn. Clerk. — How I had lost my Ship was a particular enquiry during which a Young Man appeared, who I remembered to have seen at Anamoka called Nageetee, and took a part in the Conversation expressing much pleasure at seeing me. — I now enquired after Paulehow and Feenow who they said were at Amsterdam, and Eefow agreed to accompany me there, if I would wait untill the Weather moderated. The readyness and affability of this Man gave me a high opinion of him. —

The Natives began to encrease in their Number and I observed some symptoms of a design against us, and soon after they they attempted to haul the Boat on shore. I therefore flew to Eefow with a Cutlass in my hand, when he with the other Chief called out to leave off and every thing became quiet again. —

My People who had been in the Mountains now returned

with about 3 Gallons of Water and I kept buying up the Bread fruit and other things that were brought to us. as likewise some Spears to Arm some of my Men with, as I had only 4 Cuttasses two of which were in the Boat. — As our Situation could be no Worse, I told every one I would wait untill Sun down, that by that time perhaps something might turn in our favor, and they might be induced to leave us as they had done before. — That if we attempted to go at present. we must fight our way through which we could do more advantageously at Night, and that in the Mean time we would endeavor to get off to the Boat what we had bought, — The Beach was now lined with the Natives, and we heard nothing but the knocking of Stones together which they had in each hand, which I knew very well would be the method of Attack — It being now Noon I served a Cocoa Nutt and a Breadfruit to each person for Dinner, and gave some to the Chiefs who I continued to be intimate & friendly with. — They were always anxious for me to sit down, but I as constantly refused for it occurred both to Mr. Nelson and myself that by that means they intended to seize hold of me. — My keeping therefore constantly on my Guard. and those about me. we eat our miserable dinner in some quietness. —

Fresh Gales at SE and ESE varying to NE in the latter part and a Storm of Wind. — After Dinner we began by little and little to get our things into the Boat which became troublesome on account of the Surf and I carefully watched the Motions of the Natives who I found still encreasing in Numbers, and that instead of their intention being to leave us, fires were made and places were fixed on for their residence during the Night. — Consultations were also held among them & every thing assured me we should be attacked. and I sent the Master Orders to keep the Boat well in upon the Beach when he saw us coming down that we might easily get in. —

I had my Log with me in the Cave writing up the occurrences and in sending it down it was nearly taken away but for the timely assistance of the Gunner.

Every Person who was now on Shore with me boldly took up their proportion of things and carried them to the Boat, when the Cheifs asked me if I would not stay with them all Night. I said no, I never sleep out of my Boat, but in the Morning we will again trade with You and I shall remain untill the Weather is Moderate that we may go as we have agreed to see Paulehow at Tonga-taboo. — Macca ackavow now got up and said you will not sleep on Shore, then Mattie. (which directly implies we will kill you,) and he left me. — The onset was now preparing, every one as I have described before kept knocking their Stones to-gether, and Eefow likewise quitted me. — We had now all but two or three things in the Boat, when I took Nageetee by the hand and we walked down the Beach every one in a Silent kind of horror. — When we came down Nageetee wanted me to stay to speak to Eefow, but I found he was encouraging them to the Attack, in which case if it had then begun, I determined to have killed him. and I ordered the Carpenter not to quit me untill the others were in the

Boat. — Nagectee therefore finding I would not listen to him quitted my hold and went off, and we all except one Man got into the Boat, who while I was getting on board. quitted the boats side and ran up the Beach to cast the Stern fast off. notwithstanding I heard the Master and others calling to him to return while they were hauling me out of the Water. —

I was no sooner in the Boat than the attack began by about 200 Men, this unfortunate poor Man was first knocked down. and the Stones flew like a shower of shot. — Many Men got hold of the Stern fast. and were near hauling us on shore, and would certainly have done if I had not had a Knife in my pocket to cut, we therefore hauled off to our Grapnel with every one more or less hurt. — In the course of this I saw five of the Natives about the Poor Man they had killed struggling who should get his Trowsers, and two of them were beating him about the head with Stones in their hands. — We had not time to think before, to my surprize they filled their Canoes with Stones and twelve Men came off. after us to renew the Combat. which they did so effectually as nearly to disable all of us. — Our Grapnel was foul but providence here afsisted us, as the Fluke broke and we got to our Oars and pulled to Sea, they however could paddle round us, so that we were obliged to sustain the Attack without being able to return it but with such Stones as lodged in the Boat, and in this I found we were much inferior to them. — We could not close with them because our Boat was lumbered and heavy. — I therefore adopted the expedient to throw over some Cloaths which beguiled them and they lost time In picking up, and by this means and the Night coming on they at last quitted us to reflect on our unhappy Situation. — The poor Man I lost was called Mr Norton, this was the second Voyage with me as Quarter Master, and his worthy

Character made me fell his loss very severely. — He has left an Aged Parent I am told who he supported. —

I once before sustained an Attack of this Nature with as small a Number of Men against a Multitude of Indians (after the death of Capt Cook) on the Morai at Owhyee, where I was left by Mr King, to act on the defensive as he calls it it. — Yet notwithstanding; I did not conceive that the power of a Mans Arm could throw stones from 2 to 8Lbs Weight with such force and exactness as these People did. — here unhappily I was without Arms and the Indians soon discovered it; but it was a fortunate circumstance that they did not begin the attack on us in the Cave, in that case nothing could have saved us, and we had nothing left but to dye as bravely as we could fighting close together, in which I found every One cheerfully to join me. —

It was from the appearance of such a resolution that awed them, supposing they could effect their purpose without risk after we got into the Boat. —

Taking this as a sample of their natural dispositions, there were little hopes to expect much where I was going, for I considered their good behaviour hitherto owing to a dread of our Fire Arms. which now knowing us to have none would not be the case; and that supposing our lives were safe, Our Boat, Compass. and Quadrant would be taken from us, and thereby I should not be able to return to my King and Country to give an account of the transaction. — While my mind was thus anxiously employed to consider what was best to be done as we were sailing along the west side of the Island, I was sollicited by all hands to take them towards home, and when I told them that no hopes of relief for us remained but what I might find at New Holland. untill I came to Timor. a distance of full 1200 leagues, where was a Governor, but that I had no Idea of the part of the Island the settlement was at, they all agreed to live on One Ounce of Bread p^r day and one Gill of Water. I therefore after examining what our real Stock of provisions was and recommending this as a sacred promise forever to their memory, bore away across a Sea where the Navigation is dangerous and but little Known, and in a small Boat 23 feet long from Stem to Stern, deep loaded with 18 Souls, without a single Map; and nothing but my own recollection and general knowledge of the situation of places assisted by an old Book of latitudes and longitude to guide me, in which particular I was happy to see every one better satisfied than myself. —

Our Stock of Provisions consisted of about 150 lbs of Bread, 28 Gallons of Water, 20 lbs of Pork, 3 Bottles of Wine and 5 Quarts of Rum. the difference between which and the quantity we had on leaving the Ship was principally owing to loss – A few Cocoa Nuts were in the Boat and some Breadfruit but the latter useless. —

It was about 8 oClock at Night when I bore away under a reefed Lug fore sail, and having divided into two Watches and got the Boat in a little Order, we returned God thanks for our miraculous preservation, and fully confident of his gracious support. I had a Mind more at ease than I had before felt. —

At day break the Gale encreased, the sun rose very firey and Red. a sure indication of a severe Gale. — At 8. it blew a mere Storm, and the Sea run very high, so that between the Seas the sail was becalmed, and when on the Top of the Sea. it was too much to have set, but I was obliged to carry to it for we were now in very eminent danger and distress, the sea curling over the Stern of the Boat which obliged us to bail with all our Might – a situation equally horrible perhaps was never experienced. —

Our Bread was in Bags and getting Wet, to be starved to death was therefore inevitable if it could not be prevented. — I therefore began to examine what cloaths there were in the Boat and what other things could possibly be spared, and haveing determined for only two Suits to be kept for each person, the rest was thrown overboard. which with some Rope and Spare Sails lightened the Boat considerably and We had more Room to bail the Water out. — Fortunately the Carpenter had a good Chest in the Boat, I therefore fixed on it to put the Bread in the first favorable Moment His Tool Chest also was cleared and the Tools stowed in the Bottom of the Boat, so that this became a second convenience. —

I now served a tea spoon full of Rum to each person (for we were very wet and cold) with a quarter of a Breadfruit which was scarce eatable for dinner, but our engagement was now fully to be carried into Execution, and I was sacredly determined with my life to make what provisions I had to last Eight Weeks, let the daily proportion be ever so small. —

At Noon I considered my distance from Tofoa to be 86 Miles WBN ½ N my Lat⁰ 19..27 S⁰ and Long⁰ 183..52 E.ᵗ — My intention is to steer to the WNW that I may see a Group of Islands called Fidgee if they, lie in that direction. —

Rem.s in the Bounty's Launch Monday 4.th May 1789 at Sea.

This day the Weather was very Severe, it blew a Storm from NE. to ESE – The Sea run higher than Yesterday and the fatigue of bailing to keep the Boat from filling was exceedingly great. – We could do nothing more than keep before the Sea, in the course of which the Boat performed so wonderfully well that I no longer dreaded any danger in that respect, but among the hardships we were to undergo that of being constantly Wet was not the least. – the Nights were very cold, and at day light our limbs so benumbed that we could scarce find the use of them. – At this time I served a tea spoonfull of Rum to each person which every one agreed. did him a great deal of good. –

As I have mentioned before I determined to keep to the WSW untill I got more to the Northward, for I not only expected to have better Weather, but to see those Islands called Fidgee as I have often understood from the Natives of Anamoka. that they lie in that direction, but if I recollect right Capt.r Cook considers them to be in the NW. – As I was speaking and representing the situation of these Islands as I had been told by the Natives, we descovered a Small flat Island of a moderate height. It was now Noon. The Island bearing WSW. 4 or 5 leagues. It was with great difficulty I could Observe, I however got a good latitude & found my situation to be in 18..5 S.° 182 : 16 E.t , having made a N 72 W. Course dist 95 Miles from Yesterday Noon. — I now divided five Small Cocoa Nutts for our dinners and every one was satisfied. —

Rem.ᵏ in the Bounty's Launch. Tuesday 5ᵗʰ May 1789 at Sea

Towards the Evening the Gale moderated and became a strong breeze. — The Wind SEᵗ. —

A little after Noon other Islands appeared and at 10 Min.ᵗ past 3 OClock could count eight, the Northernmost being the largest. The first Island seen bore South 4 leagues: close to which lies a high Rock. — The next Island bore S½W 5 leagues — the next bore SSW 4 leag.ˢ. the next SSW 5 leag.ˢ — the next WSW 5 leag.ˢ the next A NWBW½W 6 leag.ˢ and the Northernmost and largest Island NWBN. about 7 leagues which with the Rocky Islot close to the South of Island first seen make 9 in Number — I kept my course to the NWBW. determined to pass between the large Island and the next to the Southward. — The large Isl.ᵈ and the one first seen came in a line at NNW. and SSE in which direction they are 10 leagues apart.

At 6 OClock saw three other Islands to the WBN. of the large Island. the latter then bore NNE about 3 leagues and one to the Southward Isl.ᵈ A bearing SSW about 2 leagues, and the N Westernmost Island NW½W 7 leagues. — Off the NE part of the large Island lie 2 small Keys. — .

I now fixed on Steering WNW for the Night and stood on under a Reef'd Foresail. — Served a few broken pieces of Breadfruit for Supper and performed prayers. — The Night turned out fair and Smooth Water and having had tolerable Rest, our Spirits and Strength by the Morning seemed vastly better and we very contentedly breakfasted on a few pieces of Yams that were found in the Boat. — After breakfast we prepared a Chest for our Bread and got it secured by Noon, but unhappily a great deal was damaged and Rotten this nevertheless we were obliged to keep for Use. ——

I have hitherto been only able to keep an imperfect account of our Run, but have now got ourselves a little better equipped. and a line Marked, & having practised at counting Seconds. every one can do it with some exactness

The Land I have passed is very likely to be a part of those Islands called Fidgee. — They lie between the latitude of 19..05 S° & 18..19 S° and between the longitude of 182..02 and 181..33 E.t The largest may be about 6 Leagues in Circuit but it is impossible for me to be very exact, — to show where they are to be found again is doing a great deal in my present situation. The Sketch I have made of them will give a better Idea of their situation and Extent.— I believe all the larger Isles are inhabited as they appeared very fertile. —

At Noon I observed the latitude to be 18..10 S° and considered my Course from Yesterday to be NWBW ½ W dist 94 Miles Long.d in 180.51 E'

For dinner I served some of the Rotten Bread and a Gill of Water, Our Wants are now beginning to have a dreadfull aspect which nothing but a firm and determined resolution can fight against, a situation peculiarly miserable on a Commander. —

H	K	F	Courses	Winds	Rem.ᵈ Wednesday 6ᵗʰ May 1789. In the Bounty's Launch.
1	4		NNW.	ENE	Very hazy W.ʳ but fair
2	4				
3	4				
4	4				
5	3	4			
6	4				Hauled the Wind saw two High Islands A NWBS 6 Leagues and B
7	5	4	NBW	NEBE	NWBW 8 Leagues. — Fresh Breezes steered to Windward of the Northermost
8	5	4			Served two Cocoa Nutts for Supper —
9	5	4			
10	5	4			Bore up the Island B WBS 4 leagues.
11	5		NW.		
12	4				
1	3	4			
2	4				
3	4				
4	4		WNW.		
5	3	4			
6	3	4			The Isl.ᵈ B SSE 10 Leag.ˢ. Saw 5 others a small one C SBW 5 leagues
7	3	4	NWBN	ENE	a little larger one D NWBS½S 6 Leag.ˢ a High Mountainous one E NW
8	4		NWBN		9 Leag.ˢ. another middle size F West 3 Leag.ˢ and another G NEBE 7
9	2	2	West		or 8 Leag.ˢ Steered between those two last. —
10	4				At 7ʰ the Isl.ᵈ F bore true S.ᵒ and now proved to be two Isl.ᵈˢ with only
11	3	4			a Channel for Boats between them. — At 9ʰ 35' a Small Key H bear.ᵍ West.
12	3				At 10¾ saw a large Isl.ᵈ I SW 8 Leag.ˢ
	99		"	"	Fair W.ʳ & hazy. The Key H SEBS½E 2 Miles. The Isl.ᵈ E SBE½E 7 Leag.ˢ. the
	100				Isles F E.ᵗ 5 Leag.ˢ An Isl.ᵈ K S¾W 5 Leag.ˢ Isl.ᵈ I SSW to W.ᵗ and discovered
	2000				another large Isl.ᵈ L NBW 8 or 9 Leag.ˢ dist.ᵗ
			Meriᵈ Alt.ᵗ⊙ Center	} 56. 6	Served a half Gill of Cocoa Nutt Milk and an oz of the Meat to each
					person for Dinner. —

Course	Dist	Latitude		Longitude
		Obs.ᵈ	DR	DR
N 50 W	84	17..17 S	17..10 S	179..43 E

Journal

About 6 o'Clock this afternoon I discovered two Islands WBS 6 leagues and NWBN 8 leagues I therefore kept to Windward of the northernmost and passing it by 10 oClock I resumed my Course to the NW. and WNW. At Day light in the Morning I discovered a Number of other Islands from SSE to the West round to the NEBE between which I determined to pass At Noon when I observed, a small Key bore SEBS ½ E 2 Miles from me, and from S¾W. by the SE to East I had past 10 Islands the largest of which might be about 6 or 8 leagues in Circuit. — Much larger lands appeared in the SW. and SBW. between which I directed my Course. —

Our supper, Breakfast and dinner consisted of a Gill of Cocoa Nutt Milk and the Meat which did not exceed two ounces to each person which was received very contentedly, but we suffered drought, and I dared not land as I had no Arms and we are less capable of defending ourselves than we were at Tofoa. —

To keep an Account of the Boats run is of itself Laborious, being constantly Wet with the Sea breaking Over us, but as we advanced towards the land the sea became smoother and I was enabled to form a Sketch of the Islands which will serve to give a General knowledge of their Extent. — Those that I have been near are fruitfull and Hilly, some very mountainous and none but are of good height

To our great Joy we hooked a Fish to day but lost him miserably disapointed by it being lost in getting into the Boat! —

H	K	F	Courses	Winds	Remarks Thursday 7th May 1789 In the Bounty's Launch.
1	3		NWbN	ENE	Fair Wr and Hazy
2	3				
3	3				At 5¾ the extremes of the Isld L (set NbW at Noon) NWbW½W to NEb½E.—
4	3		WNW		Isld I on the South extending as far as SWbW. and on the N. Island L as far
5	3				as NWbW. — Could see nothing more.—
6	2	2	WbN	NE	At 6 passed over a Shoal Bank with only four feet Water on it with
7	3	6			no break — at least 6 leagt from the Shore.—
8	3	4			
9	4	4			Served a Gill of Water and an Oz of rotten Bread for Supper
10	4	4			
11	4	4			
12	4	4			
1	4				Light Squalls
2	3	4			
3	3				
4	3				At day break discovered more land. M from WbN to NbW 8 leagt distant.
5	4				a High round Hill Isld N bore NNW 6 leagt. — and I could see the land I bearg
6	3				SE to SSE — Hazy Wr
7	3		NNW		
8	3		NWbN	NEbN	At 9.30 I found we were set to the SW by a Current and could not weather the
					land in the NW — I therefore Kd but the Wind varying I got on the Northn Tack again
9	2	4	NW	NbE	Extremes SWbW½W. to NW 7 Miles off Shore.— Served a Spoonfull of Rum and
10	1		WNW	North	a bit of Bread for Breakfast —
	1		NNW	NE	At 10 Variable Wr mostly Cloudy — Two small Rocky Islots now made the N extreme
11	2	4			of the land. which we had to Weather against a lee Current setting us on ye Shore
12	2	4	"	"	Cloudy Wr with baffling Winds — We now saw two large Sailing Cannoes
					coming after us along Shore within the Islots which now bore WNW 2 Miles
					and the High Round Hill Island NEbE — Out Oars and rowed to the NW.—
					Southernmost part of the Shore SbW.—

No good observation as
we did not see the Sun come to the
Merid but an Altd I had proved
I was as far North as 16.40 So

6 Center 56..24 — Every Mile it had to rise made me more to the Northwd

Course	Dist	Obsd	Latitude DR	Longitude DR	Remks
					Latitude at Noon by protracted bearings
N56W	79	—	16..33 So	170..34 E	16..29 So

Journal

I continued my Course to the NW between the Islands which by the Evening appeared of considerable extent Woody and Mountainous. The Northernmost bore from N b W ½ W. to N E ½ E. and the Southernmost from S. to S W b W. At 6 OClock I was nearly Midway between them, and about 6 Leag⁵ distant from each Shore when I fell in on a Coral Bank where I had only 4 feet Water without the least break or ruffle of the Sea to give us Warning. — I could see that it extended about 1 Mile or 2 in Circuit; but as it is not improbable that it extends much farther I have laid it down so in my Sketch. —

     I now directed My Course N W b N for the Night and served each person an Oz of the Rotten Bread and a Gill of Water for their Supper. —

     It may readily be supposed that our Lodgings are very miserable and confined and I have it only in my power to remedy the last defect by putting ourselves at Watch and Watch so that one half is sitting up while the other has no other Bed than the Bottom of the Boat or upon a Chest. and nothing to cover us but the Heavens Our Limbs are dreadfully Cramped for we cannot Stretch them out, and the Nights are so cold and being generally very wet, we can scarce move ourselves after a few hours Sleep.

     At Dawn of Day I again discovered land from W N W to W S W and another Island N N W the latter a high round lump of but little extent, and I could see the Southern land I had passed in the Night. — Being very Cold I served a tea spoon full of Rum and a Morsel of Bread for Breakfast. — As I advanced towards the land in the West it appeared in a Variety of forms; some extraordinary high Rocks, and the Country agreeably interspersed with high and low land covered in some places with Wood, with some projecting high Clifts to the Sea, and off the N E part lay two small Rocky Islots between which & the Island to the N E 4 Leag⁵ apart I directed my Course but a lee Current very unexpectedly set me very near to the Shore, and I could only get clean of it by rowing, passing over the Reef that surrounded the Rocky Islots. — We now observe two large Sailing Cannoes coming swiftly after us along shore, and being apprehensive of their intentions we rowed with some Anxiety being too sensible of our Weak and defenceless State. — Being constantly wet it is with the utmost difficulty I can open a Book to write, & I am sensible that I can do no more than point out where these Lands are to be found. & give an Idea of their extent. —

H	K	F	Courses	Winds	Remᵏ Friday 8ᵗʰ May 1789. In the Bounty's Launch
1	3		N W	N N E	Cloudy Wʳ and light Airs. Under Oars & Sails the Cannoes in Chace.—
2	3				
3	2		‥	‥	The Cannoes left of Chace.
4	1			Calm	Heavy Rain Thunder and Lightning.—Spread our Boats Sails to catch
5	2			N E	Water and filled about 6 Gallons. besides quenching our thirst.—When
6	2				the Rain was over served an Ounce of Pork and Bread with a Gill of Water
7	2				for Supper and Dinner.—
8	2			‥	At 5¼ the Rocky Islots bore E b S ½ S. 3 leagˢ & the Extenᵗ of the Main Iˢˡᵈˢ N b E ½ E to S b E
9	5		N N W	N N E	7 or 9 leagues.— Cloudy Wʳ served a tea Spoonfull of Rum with a bit of bread being very Cold
10	5				and Wet.—
11	4	4			
12	4	4			
1	3	6			
2	3	6			
3	3	4			
4	3	4			Squally with Rain
5	3	4			
6	3	6			Fair Wʳ after a Most uncomfortable Night began to dry our Cloaths
7	3				
8	3				Served a bit of Bread and a Gill of Cocoa Nutt Milk for breakfast.—
9	3	2			
10	3				Saw a Shark and some Flying Fish but cannot catch any.—
11	3				
12	3				Fine pleasant Trade and Smooth Water—Served a ½ oz of Pork
	77				1 oz of Bread and a Gill of Cocoa Nutt Milk for dinner.— All Hands
3	70				in tolerable Spirits.—
4	40				

Course	Dist	Latitude		Longitude
		Obsᵈ	D R	D R
N 62 W	62	16°..04' S	15°..51'	177°..38' E

Journal

Untill Sun Rise the Weather was very Rainy, and in the Afternoon it was very heavy with Thunder and Lightning. — The forenoon turned out fair and we shipt oursilves, and having wrung our Cloaths we got tolerably dry. —

Only one Cannoe gained upon us and by 3 o'Clock in the Afternoon was only 2 Miles off at which time she gave over Chace. —

If I may judge from the Sail of the Vessel they are the very Same as at the Friendly Islands, and the nearness of their Situation leaves me little Room to doubt of their being the same kind of People. — Whether these Cannoes had any hostile intention against us is a matter of doubt, perhaps we might have received great relief from them, but to have known this would have insured instant death to us if their intentions had not been friendly. — Every person in our defenceless situation would most likely have done as we have. —

The Heavy Rain came on at 4 o'Clock when every person did his utmost to catch some Water, and we compleated our whole Stock to 34 Gallns besides quenching our thirst for the first time since we have been at Sea. — But an attendant consequence made us pass the Night very miserably, for being very Wet and no dry things to shift or Cover us, we experienced Cold and Shiverings scarce to be conceived. The Allowance I issued to day was 1½ oz of Pork, 1 Tea Spoon full of Rum and 2 oz. Bread, and 2 Gills of Cocoa Nutt Milk to each person. The Rum altho such a Small Quantity does us the greatest service — We have a Fishing line always out but are not so fortunate as to catch any thing notwithstanding we see a number of Fish. —

The Land I have passed Yesterday and to day is a Group of 14 or 16 Islands lying between the Latd. 16..26 S° and 17..57 S° and Longd. 178°05 Et to 180..31 East. Three of those Islands are Large having from 30 to 40 Leagues of Sea Coast. —

H	K	F	Courses	Winds	Rem.ᵈˢ Saturday 9th May 1789 In the Bountys Launch
1	2	6	NWbN	NNE	A fine Pleasant Trade and Smooth Water
2	2	2			Employed cleaning the Boat and drying Cloaths – I amused
3	2	2			all Hands by describing the Situation of New Guinea & New Holland
4	2	2			and also Timor which I drew on a piece of Paper
5	2			NE.	
6	2	4			Serv'd a Gill of Water and ½ oz of Bread for Supper. Sung a Song
7	2	4			and Went to Sleep. —
8	3				The fine Wᵣ so far revived us that every one was wonder-
9	2	6			fully in high Spirits. — Made a pair of Scales out of two Cocoa Nutt shells
10	2	4			to weigh the bread with and having Pistol Balls with us 24 of which
11	2	4			weighed a lb I adopted One as the proportion that each person should
12	2	4		EbSd	have at a time. —
1	2	4			
2	3				
3	2	4			
4	3				
5	2	2			After a fine Nights rest the day succeeded as fine and serene as before
6	3				—
7	2	7			Serv'd a Gill of Cocoa Nutt Milk for breakfast and some decayed bread
8	2	4			Saw Flying Fish and Tropic Birds
9	3				Empᵈ drying Wet Cloaths. —
10	4			NbWE	
11	3	4			
12	4				Fine Wᵣ Divided four Cocoa Nutts for our Dinners and eat the remainder
66					of the decayed bread. that we could at all put into our Mouths.
447					some pounds were so bad as to be worse than can be conceived. —
5		9	Merid.ⁿ Altᵈ ☉ Center	56. 40ˢ	

			Latitude		Longitude
Course	Disᵗ	Obs.ᵈ	DR		DR
N 75 W	64	15..47 S	15..39. S		176. 35. Eᵗ

Journal

This afternoon we got our Boat cleaned out and it took us the whole day to get every thing dry and in Order. — Hitherto I have issued the allowance by guess, but I now got a pair of Scales made with two Cocoa Nutt Shells, and having accidentally some Pistol Balls in the Boat 24 of which weighed One lb, or 16 Oz. I adopted one as the proportion of Weight that each person should receive of Bread at the times I served it. — I also amused all hands with describing the situation of New Guinea and New Holland. and I gave every information, that in case any accident happened to me, those who survived might have some Idea of what they were about, and arrive safe at Timor, which at present they knew nothing of more than the Names. —

At Night I served a Gill of Water and a ½ Oz of Bread for Supper. — In the Morning half a Gill of Cocoa Nutt Milk and some of the decayed Bread for Breakfast, and for Dinner I divided the Meat of four Cocoa Nutts with the remainder of the Rotten Bread which was worse than can well be conceived. —

H	K	F	Courses	Winds	Rem.ˢ Sunday 10ᵗʰ May 1789 In the Bounty's Launch
1	2	2	NNbN	EbN	Fine Wʳ. I now got fitted a pair of Shrouds to each Mast, and contrived
2	2	4			a Canvas Weather Cloth round the Boat also raised the Quarters about 9
3	2	6			Inches by help of the Seats, and found it of great Service
4	2	2			
5	3		"		Served a bit of bread and a Gill of Water for Supper
6	3	2			
7	3			SE	
8	3			"	Cloudy
9	3	4	NNbN	SSE	Squally much Rain Thunder and Lightning. — Caught 20 Gallˢ of Water
10	3				
11	3				
12	3			SE	Being very wet and Cold. and no Shelter. served a tea spoon full of Rum
1	3	6	NNbN		to each Man. —
2	3	6			
3	4				
4	4				
5	3	6			
6	3	6		SSE	
7	4				
8	4		"	"	Squally and Rain with a high Sea. Obliged to keep before it which
9	4		NWbN		is the cause of the Course being altered. —
10	4				Served Bread and Water for breakfast at the proportion of 2 oz of the
11	4				first and a Gill of the last to each person pʳ. day as before mentioned
12	4		"	"	Fresh Gales and Cloudy — Most uncomfortably Wet and Cold. the Sea
	83				constantly breaking over us — Cannot keep our Course. —
5	83				
5	96		Meridⁿ Altᵈ } O Center }	57.02	Served a Morsel of Pork about ½ an oz. and Bread & Water for dinner

Course	Dist	Latitude		Longitude
		Obsᵈ	DR	DR
Nb¼W	78	15..57 S	15..11 S	175..20 E

In the Afternoon I got fitted a pair of Shrouds to each Mast and contrived a Canvass Weather Cloth round the Boat and raised the quarters about 9 Inches by Nailing on the Seats of the Stern Sheets which proved of great benefit to us. —

About 9 OClock in the Evening the Clouds began to gather and we had a prodigious fall of Rain with severe Thunder and Lightning — by Midnight we caught about 20 Gallons of Water. — We were now miserably Wet and Cold, I therefore served to each person about a teaspoonfull of Rum to enable us to bear with our distressed situation without considering it, if it was possible, a point of niceifity. — but as the Weather continued extremely bad and the Wind increased, we spent a very distressing Night without Sleep but such as could be got in the midst of the Rain. — We had no relief with the day but its light — The Sea was constantly breaking over us and kept two persons bailing, and we had no Choice how to Steer for we were obliged to keep before the Waves to avoid filling the Boat. — The allowance to each person which I serve regularly at Sun set, at 8 in the Morning, and at Noon is 1/24 of a lb at each Meal. — to day I gave about 1/2 an Oz of Pork for dinner, which altho any Moderate person would have in the most plentifule situation considered in quantity as a Mouthfull; was divided into three and four. —

H	K	F	Courses	Winds	Remᵏˢ Monday 11th May 1789 In the Bountys Launch
1	4	.	NWbW½W	SSE	Fresh Gales and very Squally and a high Sea so that it is seldom
2	4				we can keep our Course which is West — Hands constantly bailing. —
3	4				
4	5				
5	4		NBN	SEBS	
6	5				Served ¹⁄₂₄ lb of Bread and a Gill of Water for Supper. —
7	5				
8	5				
9	5				
10	5				
11	5				
12	5				Very Cold and Wet constantly shipping Water and bailing. —
1	4				Carefully attending the Run of the Sea, sometimes Steering WSW
2	4				to make up for our being obliged to keep before it to the NW.
3	4				
4	3				
5	2	4		SE	
6	2	4			Cold and Wet served a tea Spoonfull of Rum and a Morsel of Bread
7	4				for Breakfast. — Limbs Crampt.
8	5				Hard Gale — Sea running frequently over our Stern and our Situation
9	5				highly dangerous. —
10	5				
11	5				
12	5				Dᵒ Wᵗʳ Sun just shewed itself at Noon — Served a ½ oz of Pork & ¹⁄₂₄ lb
	105				Bread & 1 Gill of Water for Dinner to each person. — Given many Courses from
5	9	6	Steerᵈ Allᵒ	57„14	WSW to NW but I have only set down the mean of the Whole as I cannot be more
7	2	1	O Center		exact. —

			Latitude		Longitude
Course	Distᵗ	Obsᵈ	DR	DR	
N71W	102	14..50 S	14..44 S	173..41 E	

Journal

Strong Gales and very Squally Wr with a high breaking Sea, so that we are miserably Wet and suffer great cold in the Night. In the Morning at day break I served to every person about a teaspoonfull of Rum. our Limbs being so crampt as hard to feel the use of them. Our situation was now highly dangerous the Sea frequently running over our Stern which kept us bailing with all our Strength.— At Noon the Sun Appeared which gave us as much pleasure as in a Winters day in England Our Miserable allowance as Yesterday.—

H	K	F	Courses	Winds	Rem.s Tuesday 12th May 1789 In the Bountys Launch
1	4	4	West	SE	Strong Gale and a high Sea frequently breaking over us — Hands
2	4	4			constantly bailing the Water out
3	4	4			
4	4	4			
5	4				
6	4				Served 1/24 lb Bread and a Gill of Water for Supper.
7	4	2			
8	4	4			
9	4	4			
10	4	4			
11	4	4			
12	4	4			Fresh Gale can keep our Course pretty steadily, bearing up to the NW.
1	3	4			only every five or ten Minutes when the Sea runs remarkably high,
2	3	4			which I make up for by Steering more to the Southward when we can
3	3	4			
4	3	4			
5	3	4			Constant Rain and very cold. — One Man Ill of the Cholick — Served
6	3	4		NNE	a tea spoonfull of Rum and a Morsel of Bread. — Our situation now
7	3	4			in every respect truly Miserable. — Limbs very much Crampt.
8	3	4			
9	2	6			Moderate Breezes and Cloudy Wr with Rain
10	2	4		Varia.	
11	1	4			
12	1				Calm and Cloudy. — Most of us complaining of a violent Shivering. —
	89				Served 1/24 lb Bread and a Gill of Water for dinner. — No Sun — Saw Fish
701					but cannot catch any. — Some Tropic Birds. — Our Cloaths will not dry.
790					

			Latitude		Longitude
Course	Dist	Obs°	DR		DR
WbN	89	none	14..33 S		872..55 E

Journal

Having again experienced a dreadfull Night of it, the day showed to me a poor Miserable set of Beings full of Wants but nothing to releive them. — Some complained of a great pains in their Bowels and all of having but little use of their Limbs. — What Sleep we got was scarce refreshing being covered with Sea and Rain, and two persons were always obliged to keep bailing — I served my tea spoonfull of Rum at day dawn as usual, and 1/24 of a lb of Bread with a Gill of Water for Supper, Breakfast and Dinner. —

At Noon almost Calm and no sun to be seen — Some of us shivering with Cold. — the direction of my Course is to pass to the Northward of the New Hebrides

H	K	F	Courses	Winds	Remks. Wednesday 13th May 1789. In the Bountys Launch
1		4	W	SE	Dark Cloudy Wr. and a very moist air
2		4			
3		4	NW.	Southerly	
4		4			Saw a Fruit on the Water which Mr. Nelson knew to be the Barringtonia
5	3		WBN	SWBS	of Forster.—
6	3		–	..	Served 1/24 of a lb of Bread. and a Gill of Water for Supper.—
7	4	2	W	So	
8	4	2			
9	5				
10	4	2			
11	5				
12	4	2		SSE	Very Squally Weather constantly shipping Water and miserably
1	3	6			Wet and Cold.
2	3	2			
3	3	4	W½S		
4	3	4			
5	3	2			
6	3		W½N	So	
7	4				
8	3	4	–	..	Served 1/24 of a lb of Bread and a Gill of Water for breakfast
9	3	6			Saw Men of War Birds and some of the same kind of fruit as
10	4		WBN	SBW	seen in the Afternoon.
11	4				
12	4		..	..	Do. Wr. and the Sun appearing at times.— Served 1/24 of a lb of Bread
	79				and a Gill of Water for Dinner— Always bailing, and very Wet.—
7	90				Got a tolerable Observation.—
Mbg			Merid. Altd. ☉ Center	57°.16'	

Course	Dist.	Latitude Obs.d	Latitude DR	Longitude DR
WbN	79	14°..57' S	14°..17' S	170°..52' E

Journal

As I saw no prospect of our getting our Cloaths dryed; I recommended it to every one to strip and wring them through the Salt Water, by which means they received, a Warmth that while wet with Rain they could not have, and be more exempt from Catching Cold and violent Rheumatic complaints.

In the afternoon we saw a kind of Fruit on the Water which Mr Nelson knew to be the Barringtonia of Forster, and as we met with the Same in the Morning and some Men of War Birds I was led to beleive we were not far from Land —

We continued constantly shipping Seas and bailing and very Wet & Cold in the Night; but I could not afford the allowance of Rum at day break The 1/24 of a lb of Bread and a Gill of Water I served as usual. —

H	K	F	Courses	Winds	Rem.ᵈ Thursday 14ᵗʰ May 1789 in the Bounty's Launch.
1	4	-	N.W.ᵗ	S.b.W.	Fresh Breezes and Cloudy – This Afternoon got our Cloaths tolerably dry
2	4		N.W.b.S	Sᵒ	
3	4				
4	4				
5	4				
6	4		"	"	Served ¹⁄₂₄ of a lb of Bread and a Gill of Water for Supper to each person
7	4				
8	4		"	"	Wind freshening and Shipping water so that we are all Wet again.
9	4				
10	4				
11	4				
12	4		"	"	Cold and Wet.
1	3	6	West	S.b.W.	
2	4				
3	4				
4	3	6			
5	3	6			
6	3	4	"	"	Saw Islands. O from S.W.b.S. 8 leagˢ to P N.W.b.W ¾ W. 6 leagˢ – Q the largest
7	4	4	N.W.b.N		with two remarkable Hills N.W.b.S ¾ S. 7 leagˢ and a Smaller Island with a
8	4	4	"	S.E	high Sugar Loaf Peak W ¾ S. 4 or 5 leagˢ –
9	4	4			Served ¹⁄₂₄ lb of Bread and a Gill of Water for Breakfast
10	4	4	N.W.b.W		
11	4	4			
12	5	-	W.N.W	"	Open Cloudy Wʳ The Sugar Loaf Peak and Islᵈ P in one at S½ E. disᵗ from
	100				Islᵈ P. 4 leagˢ – Islᵈ Q SSW½ W. – We now discovered a rocky Key N.W.b.N
	86	9			4 leagˢ and another Islᵈ R West about 8 leagˢ the whole being Six in Number.
	96	9	Mendᵈ Altᵈ		Land fertile and Woody. – Islᵈ O not in Sight. – Steered for Islᵈ R. –
			O Center ⎰ 57..49		Served ¹⁄₂₄ lb of Bread and a Gill of Water for Dinner. –

Course	Disᵗ	Satitude Obsᵈ	D.R.	Longitude D.R.	
N.63 W	89	13..29 S	13..40 S	169..31 E	

Journal

Constantly shipping Water and very Wet suffering much Cold and Shivering in the Night — Served the usual allowance of 1/24 lb Bread and a Gill of Water three times a day. —

At 6 In the Morning I discovered Islands from SWbS 3 leagues to NWbW 3/4 6 leagues which I soon after found to be four all of them high and remarkable. — At Noon I discovered a Rocky Key NWbN 4 leagues and another Island West 8 leagues so that the whole were 6 in Number, the four I had first seen bearing from S 1/2 E to SWbS distant 3 leagues from the nearest Island.

H	K	F	Courses	Winds	Rem.ᵏˢ Friday 15ᵗʰ May 1789 – Bountys Launch.
1	5		W.	SE	Fresh Gale and dark Gloomy Wʳ
2	5				
3	5		WBN		
4	5		"	"	I was abreast of the Isᵗ. R bearing SBE about a league: Sugar Loaf Peak
5	4	3	WSW		Island SE½E and North Rocks NE½N about 4 or 5 leagˢ – The Island Q SSE
6	4				and East – Island P SEBE. – Saw Smokes. –
7	4		"	"	A great deal of Sea. – Constantly Wet and Bailing – Served ¹⁄₂₄ lb Bread
8	4	6			and a Gill of Water for Supper. –
9	4	2			
10	5				
11	4	2			
12	5				
1	5		"	"	Saw another Island. S tolerably high WSW 5 leagᵗ disᵗ. –
2	5				
3	5				
4	4	4			
5	6		"	"	Fresh Gales and Squally with much Rain, but not so heavy as to be able
6	5				to collect any –
7	4	6	"	"	The Island. S seen at 1 oClock. NE 7 leagˢ. – Very Wet and Cold Sea
8	4	4			constantly breaking over us which keeps One person bailing without the
9	5		WBS		least intermission. – Served ¹⁄₂₄ lb Bread and a Gill of Water for Breakfast. –
10	4	4			
11	4	6			
12	5	.	"	"	The Rain now abated. – Gannets, Boobies, Noddies and Men of War Birds
114					Got a Sight of the Sun but apprehend it had more to rise, if so I am
96 9					more to the Northwᵈ as my Account shews. –
100 3			O.Center	57.09	Served ¹⁄₂₄ lb Bread and a Gill of Water for Dinner. –

			Latitude		Longitude
Course	Disᵗ	Obsᵈ	DR	DR
S 80 W	113	13..55 S	13..48 S	167..35 E

Journal

Fresh Gales and Gloomy Wr. with Rain. the Sea running high & keeps us constantly bailing. —

At 4 in the Afternoon I passed the Westermost Island. — At 1 in the Morning I discovered another bearing W.N.W. 5 leagues dist. — Saw a number of Gannets Boobies and Men of War Birds. — The Situation of this last Island is in Lat. 13..29 S. Long. 160..15 E. the others lie between the latitude of 13..16 S. and 14..10 S. and between the Long. of 169..03 E. and 169..29 E. — The largest Island may have 20 leagues of Sea Coast the others about 5. or 6: The Easternmost is the smallest Island and most remarkable having a Sugar Loaf Hill. —

But very little reflection will show our miserable Situation — We are now but little better than Starving with plenty in View, yet the risk was so great to get that relief, that prolonging of life even in the midst of misery is preferable while we have hopes of surmounting all our hardships. — but for my own part I consider the general run of Cloudy and Wet Weather to be a providential blessing to us — Hot Weather would have caused us to have died raving Mad with thirst, yet now altho we Sleep covered with Rain or Sea we suffer not that dreadful Calamity. —

As I have nothing to assist my memory I cannot determine whether these Islands I have passed are part of the Hibrides or not, they are however Fertile and Inhabited for I saw several Smokes. —

H	K	F	Course	Winds	Rem.ᵈ Saturday 16ᵗʰ May 5789. In the Bounty's Launch
1	5	4	WSW	SE	Fresh Gale and much Sea with Squalls of Rain
2	5	6			
3	6				
4	5	4			
5	5	4	WbS		
6	5		WSW	..	Served 1/24 lb Bread and a Gill of Water. Sea Constantly breaking over us
7	4	6			
0	4	2	"	..	Dark dismal Night no Stars to see to steer by only the Wind to direct
9	4		WbN.		us
10	3				
11	2				
12	4	4			
1	4	6			
2	4	2			
3	4				
4	4		WSW.	SEbS	
5	4				
6	4	3			
7	3	1	..	..	Dark Cloudy Wʳ with Squalls of Rain, but not so much Wind.
0	3	1			High breaking Sea.
9	3	4			Served 1/24 lb Bread and a Gill of Water for breakfast. —
10	3	4			
11	4				
12	4		"	..	Fair Wʳ & Cloudy — Got our Cloaths to dry — Got a good Observation — Saw
	105				a Booby. Noddies and a Mother Carys Chicken. —
10	33				Served 1/24 lb of Bread and a Gill of Water & I advanced to day about 1oz of
11	50		Merid.ⁿ Alt.ᵒ ⊙ Center }	ᵒ 57..17	Pork to each person. —

Course	Disᵗ	Latitude		Longitude
		Obs.ᵒ	DR	DR
N 52 W	101	13..33 S°	13..53 S	167..35 E

Journal

Fresh Gales and Rainy W.r — The Night was dark and dismal Not a Star to be seen to Steer by and the Sea breaking constantly over us.. I find it necessary to act as much as possible against these Southerly Winds lest I be drove too near New Guinea, for in general we are drove so much before the Sea, unless at moderate intervals I was to keep my course up more to the Southward to prevent my falling in with that Coast, we should inevitably from a continuance of their Gales be thrown in sight of it, in which case most probably an End to our Voyage would soon be the consequence. —

In addition to our miserable allowance of 1/24 lb of Bread and and a Gill of Water. I Issued to day for dinner about an oz of Pork to each Person I am often sollicited for this Pork, but I consider it better to give it in ever so small quantities than use all at once or twice, which would be the case if I would allow it. —

H	K	F	Courses	Winds	Rem.ˢ Sunday 17ᵗʰ May 1789 In the Bountys Launch
1	4	..	SWbW.	SEbS	Strong Breezes and Cloudy
2	4		SW.		
3	4	6			
4	4	4			
5	4	6			
6	5		.	..	Served 1/24 lb of Bread and a Gill of Water for Supper
7	3	4			
8	3	4			
9	3	4			
10	3	4			
11	3	4	.	..	Storms of Thunder Lightning and heavy Rain – Two people constantly
12	3	4			bailing and so dark scarce able to see each other – No Stars to be seen so
1	4	4			that our Steerage is very uncertain. —
2	4	4			
3	4	4			
4	4	6			
5	5				
6	5				
7	4		..	..	Dᵒ Wʳ Very Wet and Cold. and our Situation truly unhappy
8	4				
9	4				
10	3	4			
11	3	4			
12	4		"	"	Dᵒ Wind & Rain and Sky dreadfully black and threatning a continuance
100					A Water Spout very near on board of us. — Served 1/24 lb Bread & a Gill of Water
1180					and being very Wet and Cold I gave an Oz of Pork for Dinner to each person. —
1288					Often Washing and Wringing our Cloaths out of the Salt Water for Warmth

			Latitude	Longitude	
Course	Disᵗ	Obs.ᵈ	DR	DR	
WbW	100	None	14..11 Sᵒ	164..57. Eᵗ	

Journal

Our Sun shine was of short duration Strong Breezes and dark Gloomy W^r with Storms of Thunder Lightning and Rain added to our distresses this day, and the Night was truly horrible and not a Star to be seen, so that our Steerage was uncertain At dawn of day I found every person complaining, and some of them solliciting extra allowance, but I positively refused it. — Our Situation is truly miserable — Always Wet and suffering extreme Cold in the Night without the least Shelter from the Weather — Constantly bailing to keep the Boat from filling is perhaps not an evil to us as it gives exercise, it is however a difficult thing to believe in our Situation. The little Rum I have is of great avail to us, when our Nights are peculiarly distressing I issue a teaspoonfull to each person, which is always joyfull tidings when they hear of my intentions. — At Noon a Water Spout was very near on board of us. — I issued an ounce of Pork in addition to the allowance of Bread and Gill of Water but before we begun to eat every person Stripea and Wrung their Cloaths through the Sea Water which we found Warm and refreshing. — The Sun is as much hid from us as in a Winters day in England.

H	K	F	Courses	Winds	Rem^s Monday May 18th 1789 In the Bountys Launch
1	1		SW.	East.	Light Winds and heavy Rain which enables us to keep our Stock of
2	2				Water up. —
3	3	7		SE B E	
4	4		..	..	Fresh Gale and very Squally. A heavy Sea from the SE. constantly breaking
5	4	4			over us. Two Men bailing. —
6	4		..	..	Very Wet and Cold. Served 1/24 lb. Bread & Water for Supper.
7	5				
8	5				
9	5				
10	6				
11	5	4		SE	
12	5		..	..	Dark dismal Night No Stars. Steering as the Sea directs us — Very
1	5				heavy Rain which cramps all our Limbs. —
2	5				
3	5				
4	5				
5	4	6			
6	5				
7	4	6		East	
8	4	4		SE	Rain abated Striped Naked as usual. and washed and Wrung our Cloaths
9	5				out of Salt Water. which refreshed us Wonderfully. — Served 1/24 lb Bread
10	4	6			& Water for breakfast. —
11	3	4		E	
12	3	4		E N E	Squally with Rain. Served 1/24 lb of Bread. and a Gill of Water for dinner
	106				Every one now complains of Violent pains in their Bones — Constantly
120					bailing. — Boobies - Noddies and many Tropic Gulls about. —
13	9	4			
			Merid^n Alt^d		
			☉ Center ⦆		

		Latitude	Longitude
Course	Dis^t	Obs^d	D.R.	D.R.
WSW.	106	None	14..52.S	162..35 E^t

Journal

Fresh Gales with Rain and dark dismal Night, the Sea constantly breaking over us, and nothing but the Wind and Sea to direct our Steerage. — I have now fully determined to make New Holland to the Southward of Endeavour Streights, sensible I must keep my Situation so as to make a Southerly Wind a fair One and to range along the Reefs untill I can find an Opening, within which I must find Smooth Water and the sooner pick up some Refreshments

In the Morning the Rain abated when we strived and wrung our Cloaths through the Sea Water as usual which refreshed us wonderfully. —

Every person now complained of violent pain in their Bones. — I am only surprized that I have no one yet laid up. — Served 1/24 lb Bread and a Gill of Water for Supper, Breakfast and Dinner as customary. — Constantly Bailing. —

Saw many Boobies and Noddies a Sign of being in the neighbourhood of Land. —

H	K	F	Courses	Winds	Rem Tuesday 19th May 1789 In the Bountys Launch.

H	K	F	Courses	Winds	Remₖ Tuesday 19th May 1789 In the Bountys Launch.
1	3	6	WBS	ENE	Squally with Rain
2	4	6			
3	5				A very confused Sea which breaks over us on all sides constantly bailing
4	4	4			
5	4	4	West.		
6	4	4		NE	Dark Cloudy Wr and fresh breezes Washed and Wrung our Cloaths in Salt
7	4	4			Water — Served 1⁄24 lb Bread and a Gill of Water for Supper
8	4	4			
9	4				
10	4				
11	4		..	..	Squally with Rain
12	2	6		ENE	
1	3		..	..	Constant heavy Rain and Lightning
2	3				
3	3				
4	3			..	Miserably Cold.
5	3	4			
6	4	4			
7	4	4			
8	4	4		..	Rain abated — Wrung our Wet Cloaths, when I served 1⁄24 lb Bread
9	4				and a Gill of Water for Breakfast.
10	4		"	..	Squalls
11	4			ESE to	
12	4			ENE.	Fresh Gale and Constant Rain. — I served an 1⁄2 oz of Pork to day
	97				with the Bread & Water for dinner which was thought a Feast. —
153	94				Severe Bone Achs. — All Night and day constantly bailing. —
149	1				

			Latitude		Longitude	
Course	Dist	Obs.ᵈ	DR		DR	
N 81 W.	95	None	14..37 S		166..50 E	

Journal

We past this day miserably Wet and Cold. Covered with Rain and Sea, which we could only act against at intervals by pulling of our Cloaths and wringing them through the Sea Water. — In the Night we had very severe Lightning, but otherwise so dark we could scarce see each other. The Morning produced to me many complaints on the Severity of the Weather, and I would gladly have issued my allowance of Rum if it had not appeared to me that we were to suffer much more, and that it was necessary to preserve the little I had to give relief at a time when less able to bear such hardships, but to make up, I issued about an half ounce of Pork to each person with the allowance of 1/24 lb of Bread and a Gill of Water for Dinner — All Night and day bailing without intermission. —

H	K	F	Courses	Winds	Rem.^s Wednesday 20th May 1789 In the Bountys Launch
1	3	4	West	E.N.E	Moderate and Rainy W^r
2	3	4			
3	3				
4	2	4	..	..	Deluge of Rain — Constantly bailing
5	3				
6	3		..	..	Served 1/24 lb of Bread for Supper — Water we want none for our thirst
7	2	6			seems to be quenched through our Skin. —
8	4				
9	3	2			
10	3	2			
11	3	2			
12	3	2	..	..	No intermission of Rain and at times a Deluge. —
1	3	2			
2	4				
3	3	6			
4	5				
5	4		..	..	At Dawn of day some of my people half dead. the Weather continuing
6	4				the Same. I now served two tea spoonfulls of Rum to each person.
7	4				
8	4				
9	3	4			
10	2	4			
11	2	4	..	..	Tropic Gulls Men of War Birds and Boobies
12	3		..	..	Towards Noon the Rain abated and had the Sun out Hung up our
92					Wett things to dry — Served 1/24 lb of Bread and 2 Gills of Water for
149					Dinner
1573			Meridⁿ Alt^d ⊙ .. ., ⊙ Center } 34..54		

Course	Dis^t	Latitude		Longitude	
		Obs^d	DR	DR	
N 88° W	81	14..49 S	14..40 S	159..34 E^t	

Journal

Constant heavy Rain and at times a deluge – Always Bailing. –
At Dawn of day some of my People half dead. – Our appearances were horrible, and I could look no way but I caught the Eye of some one – Extreme hunger is now evident, but thirst no one suffers or have we an Inclination to drink that desire being satisfied through our Skin. – What little Sleep we get is in the midst of Water, and we wake with Severe Cramps and Pains in the Bones. – This morning I served two tea Spoonfulls of Rum to each person and the allowance of 1/24 lb of Bread as Usual. – At Noon the Sun shone out and revived every one. –

H	K	F	Courses	Winds	Rem^s Thursday 21st May 1789 In the Bounty's Launch.
1	3	..	West	ENE	Fresh Breezes and Cloudy
2	3	4			
3	3	6	..	..	Constant Rain — Many Birds. — Boobies. Noddies and Tropic Gulls
4	4	4			flying close round us — Many Sharks, Dolphins and other Fish but
5	4	4			cannot catch any. —
6	4		..	..	Served 1/24 lb Bread for Supper as usual to each person. —
7	4				
8	4		..	..	Fresh Gale and Rain.
9	4				
10	4		..	..	A Very heavy Storm of Rain and dismal dark Weather. Our
11	4				Compass no use to us by Night and we are obliged to steer as the Wind
12	4				and Sea directs us. —
1	3	6			
2	3	6	..	..	The Deluge of Rain was now so heavy that it was with much
3	3	4	..		difficulty we could keep the Boat free. —
4	4				
5	4				
6	4		..	..	At Dawn of day the Rain Moderated a little. Served a tea spoon
7	5				full of Rum to each person —
8	5		..	~	Served 1/24 lb of Bread and Water for Breakfast as usual — every one
9	5				miserably Wet and Cold. and much distressed. —
10	5		~	~	The Weather a little better. —
11	5				
12	5		~		Fresh Gales and Cloudy W^r free of Rain with the Sun out at times,
	100				but the Sea every five Minutes breaking over us. so that we never
	1873				can omitt bailing — Served 1/24 lb of Bread and Water for dinner
	1873		Mean Alt^d ⊙ Center } 55..16		

			Latitude		Longitude
Course	Dis	Obs^d	D.R.	D.R.	
S 70 W	99	14..29 S	14..23 S	157..55 E	

Journal

Our Distresses are now extremely great we are covered with Rain and Sea that we can scarce see or make use of our Eyes — Sleep altho we long for it is horrible — for my part I seem to live without it. — We suffer extreme cold and every one dreads the approach of Night — About 2 O'Clock in the Morning we experienced a most extreme deluge of Rain — it fell so heavy that we were afraid of a dangerous tendency to the Boat and were obliged to bail with all our might. — it continued untile Dawn of Day When I served a large Allowance of Rum. — Towards Noon the Rain abated and the Sun came out, but we were miserably Wet and Cold the sea breaking constantly over us. —

H	K	F	Courses	Winds	Remks Friday 22nd May 1789 In the Bountys Launch
1	5	2	N½E	ESE	Strong Gales and fine Wr. but the Sea running very high from the NE
2	5	2			Keeps us constantly bailing and Wet. —
3	5		NBE		
4	4	4			
5	4	6			
6	4	6	-	~	The Sun set in heavy Clouds and Wetting so that we again expect Wet
7	5	4	NW½N		Weather — Served 1/24 lb of Bread. and a Gill of Water for Supper.
8	5	4			
9	5	4	~	..	Several heavy Seas broke over us and near filling the Boat Obliged
10	5	4			to carry Sail yet tremble every minute for losing my Mast. —
11	5	4			
12	5	4	~	~	Very Wet. but no Cold as when it Rains - Very dark Night
1	5	4			
2	5	4			
3	5	4			
4	5	4			
5	5	4			
6	5	4	..	SE	Very Squally with a very hard Gale. We take the Course of the
7	5	4			Sea which happuly keeps a Western direction —
8	5	4			Served 1/24 lb of Bread and a Gill of Water for Breakfast
9	5	4	NW½S	SBE	
10	5	4		SE	
11	5	4	NBN	SBE	
12	5	4	..	ESE	Fair Wr but no abatement of the Gale or Sea. — Keeping right
	191				before it and the foam running over our quarters. — With great
1675					difficulty and being propped up I got an Observation
1884					Served 1/24 lb Bread and a Gill of Water for Dinner. —
	Memo Alt O Center 55..57				

Course	Dist	Latitude		Longitude
		Obs?	DR	DR
N85W	130	14..57 S	14..12 S	155..42 Et

Journal

Our Situation to day highly perilous. — If ever Men experienced the power and goodness of Divine providence we do at this instant in a most emminent degree, and I presume to say our present situation would make the boldest Seaman tremble that ever lived — We are obliged to take the Course of the Sea running right before it and breaking all over us — Watching with the utmost Care, as the least Error in the Helm would in a Moment be our destruction — As we suffered not such Cold as when Wet with the Rain I only issued 1/24 lb Bread and a Gill of Water to each Meal. — At Noon it blew very hard and the foam of the Sea kept running over our Stern and Quarters, I however got propped up and made an Observation. —

H	K	F	Courses	Winds	Remᵏˢ Saturday 23ᵈ May 1789 In the Bountys Launch.
1	5	..	NWbN	SSE	Strong Gales and fair Wʳ. but a high breaking Sea. which keeps us
2	5				constantly bailing and Wet.
3	5		"	Sᵒ	
4	5				
5	5		West		
6	5		"	..	Served 1/24 ℔ Bread and a Gill of Water for Supper
7	5		"	..	
8	5		"	..	Hard Squalls and Rain
9	6		NWbN	SE	
10	6		"	..	The Sea flying over us with great force. Constantly bailing, Dismal
11	5	4	NNW	EbS	dark Night—
12	5				
1	5		NWbN	SSE	
2	5				
3	5				
4	5	4	West	SE	
5	4		..	..	At Dawn of day I found every one in a most distressed condition
6	3	4			Served two tea spoonfulls of Rum to each person & the Rain being
7	5				over every one wrung their Wet cloaths through Salt Water
8	5		W½N		Served 1/24 ℔ Bread & a Gill of Water for Breakfast. —
9	5		"	SSE	
10	5		..	Sᵒ	
11	4	6	NWbN	SE	
12	5		..	..	Fair Wʳ but very little abatement of the Gale and the Sea equally
	119				high — Served 1/24 ℔ Bread & a Gill of Water for Dinner — Constantly
	1604				Wet & bailing. Every one has severe Bone Achs — With great difficulty
	1723		Meridᵈ Altᵈ		I got an Observation. —
			ʘ Center }	55..30	

Course		Disᵗ	Latitude		Longitude
			Obsᵈ	DR	DR
N87¼W		116	13..44 S	13..30 S	153..40 E

Journal

The Misery of this day has exceeded the preceeding — The Night was dreadfull
The Sea flew over us with great force and kept us bailing with horror and anxiety. —
. At Dawn of day I found every one in a most distressed situation, and I now began
to fear that another such night would produce the End of several who were no longer able
to bear it. — Every one complained of Severe Bone Achs which was cured in some Measure
by about two Spoonfulls of Rum, and having wrung our Cloaths and taken our break=
=fast of Bread and Water we became a little refreshed. — Towards Noon it came fair
but very little abatement of the Gale. and the Sea equally high — With great difficulty
I got an Observation. —

H	K	F	Course	Winds	Rem: Sunday 24ʰ May 1789 In the Bounty's Launch
1	5	4	NNW	NNE	Strong Gale and very high Sea Constantly Wet and bailing. —
2	5	2			
3	5	2	..	..	Many Mother Carey's Chickens —
4	5		..	..	Gale moderating and Sea less. – So that I am able to Steer more across it
5	4	6			
6	4	6	..	..	Weather looking much better which rejoices all hands. – Served ¹⁄₂₄ lb
7	5				Bread and a Gill of Water for Supper.
8	4	4			
9	5				
10	4	6			
11	5				
12	5		..	..	Fresh Gale and a fine Night but being Wet with the Sea we Suffered
1	5				Cold. —
2	5				
3	5				
4	5				
5	5				
6	5		..	..	Fine Morning and I had the pleasure to see every ones countenance
7	4	4			bear the marks of more life and Spirit than I expected. – Served
8	4				¹⁄₂₄ lb Bread and a Gill of Water for breakfast and hung up all our
9	4	2			Wet Cloaths which are now become so thread bare that they neither keep
10	4	2			out Cold or Wet.
11	4	4			
12	5		..	..	Fine Wr and for the first time these 15 days past we found a little warmth
117					from the Sun – I now Served an oz of Pork with the usual allowance
19	23				of Bread and Water for Dinner. —
20	40				

			Latitude		Longitude	
Course	Disᵗ	Obsᵈ		DR	DR	
N 84 W	114	13.. 33 S	13.. 33 S		151.. 52 Eᵗ	

Journal.

Towards Evening the Weather looked much better and rejoiced all hands so that they eat their miserable allowance with more satisfaction than for some time past. — The Night also was fair but being always Wet with the Sea we suffered Cold, but a fine Morning I had the pleasure to see produce some chearfull countenances — Towards Noon the Weather improved and for the first time for 15 days past we found a little Warmth from the Sun. — We stript & hung our Cloaths up to dry which are now become so thread bare that they will neither keep out Wet or Cold. — With the usual allowance of Bread and Water for dinner I served an Oz of Pork to each person. —

H	K	F	Courses	Winds	Remks Monday 25th May 1789 In the Bountys Launch
1	4	6	WBS	SSE	Fine Wr and fresh Gale. the Sea running fair and not breaking
2	4				which is a great relief to us. —
3	4				Many Birds — Boobies — Noddies and Men of War Birds
4	4		..		Examined the Bread.
5	4	4			
6	4	4			
7	4	4			
8	4	4			
9	4	4			
10	4	4			
11	5				
12	5				
1	4				
2	4				
3	4	4			
4	4	4			
5	4				
6	4			..	Served 1/24 lb of Bread and a Gill of Water for Breakfast
7	5				
8	4	4			
9	5				
10	5				
11	5				
12	5		..	..	Fair Wr & Squally Tropic Gulls and Noddies. Caught a Noddy by hand
110					it is about the Size of a Small Pigeon this was a Small help to us — I divided
2040					it with its entrails into 18 Portions and with 1/24 lb of Bread we made
2150			Merid Alt O Center } 55..20S		our dinners using Salt Water as Sauce. —

Course	Dist	Latitude		Longitude
		Obd	DR	DR
N ¼ N	108	13..32 S	13..32 S	150..01 Et

This afternoon we had many Birds about which are never far from land such as Boobies and Noddies. —

About 3 OClock the Sea began to run fair and we shipped but little Water. I therefore determined to know the exact quantity of bread I had according to my present Issues, and on examining it found I had 29 days allowance. — In the course of this time I hoped to be at Timor, but as that was very uncertain, and perhaps after all be Obliged to go to Java. I determined to proportion my Issues to 6 Weeks. — I considered this would be ill received; it therefore demanded my most determined reso= lution to inforce it provided I was opposed, for small as the quantity was I intended to take away for our future good, yet it appeared like robbing them of life, and some who were particularly Voracious would not like it — I how ever represented it so essentially Necessary to guard against delays on our Voyage by contrary Winds or other causes, and I promised to enlarge upon the allowance as we got on; that it was readily agreed to. I therefore fixed that every person should receive 1/24 lb for Breakfast and 1/24 lb for Dinner. so that by omitting the Issue at Supper I should have 43 days Allowance. —

At Noon we caught a Noddy by hand. — It is about the size of a Small Pigeon — I divided it with its entrails into 18 portions and by the method of Who shall have this? it was issued with the allowance of Bread for dinner, and eat bones and all with Salt Water for Sauce. — Some of my people begin to exhibit great marks of Weakness and complain of want of evacuation by Stool. —

H	K	F	Courses	Winds	Rem.ˢ Tuesday 26ᵗʰ May 1789. In the Bountys Launch.
1	5		W b S	SS E.	Fair W.ʳ with a fresh Gale and Squally with Rain at times. —
2	5				
3	5				
4	5				
5	5		~	~	Caught a Booby by hand several flying about us almost lighting
6	5				on our heads. — I directed it to be killed for Supper when the blood
7	5				was given to three of the most distressed for food. The body entrails
8	5				beak & legs I divided into 18 pieces and with a Small allowance of
9	5				bread we made a Chearfull Supper.
10	5				
11	5				
12	5				
1	4				
2	4	4			Moon changed this Morning. —
3	5				
4	4	4			
5	4				Very fine W.ʳ which has increased my peoples Spirits.
6	4				Caught another Booby. — Served 1⁄24 lb of Bread and a Gill of
7	4			S.E.	Water for breakfast.
8	4				
9	4				Tropic Gulls. Boobies Noddies and many pieces of Trees passing
10	4	4			some Covered with Barnacles. —
11	4	4			
12	4	4	~	~	Fine W.ʳ — Served 1⁄24 lb. Bread and divided the Bird as in the Evening
	112				into 18 parcels.
2	80				
22	62		Merid Alt.ᵈ ⟩ O Center ⟩	55.. 0	

		Latitude		Longitude
Course	Dis.ᵗ	Obs.ᵈ	DR	DR
S 85 W	112	13.. 41 S	13.. 37 S	140.. 07 E.ᵗ

Journal

In the Evening we saw several Boobies, and flying so near to us that we caught one of them by hand. — This Bird is as large as a Good Duck it has got its Name from Seamen for suffering itself to be caught on the Masts and Yards of Ships — They are generally in the Neighbourhood of Land. — I directed it to be killed for Supper and the blood was given to three of the most distressed for want of food. — The body Entrails. Beak and feet I divided into 18 Shares and with an allowance of Bread which I made a Merit of granting we made a good Supper. —

In the Morning we caught another Booby so that Providence seems to be relieving our Wants in a very extraordinary Manner. — Towards Noon we passed a great many pieces of the branches of Trees. some of which appeared to have been a longtime in the Water —. I got a good Observation for the Latitude. — Every person being overjoyed at the addition to our Dinner which I distributed as I had done in the Evening. giving the Blood to those who were the most in Want of food. — To make our Bread a little savory. we frequently dip it in salt Water, but for my part. I always break it into small pieces and eat it in my allowance of Water in a Cocoa Nutt Shell. with a Spoon taking care never to take but a piece at a time so that I am as long at dinner as at a more plentifull. Meal. ——

H	K	F	Courses	Winds	Rem.ˢ Wednesday 27ᵗʰ May 1789 In the Bounty's Launch
1	4		West	SE	Fine Wʳ – I think Monsʳ Bougainville was about this Track in the
2	4				month of June and had Weather very like to what I have experienced – It
3	4				also runs to the Eastᵈ of the Friendly Islands but from 100 leagˢ to the
4	4				Eastᵈ of them to Otaheite and to the Easterᵈ the Weather in these months is
5	4	4			more Serene and Settled –
6	4	6		ESE	At 6 Caught another Booby, The Blood eat by those who were the weakest
7	4	4			The Maw contained several Small Flying Fish & squids all of which I ordered
8	4	4			to be kept for dinner –
9	4	4			
10	4	4			
11	4	4			
12	4				
1	4	4			
2	4				
3	3	6			
4	4				
5	3	6			
6	5	4			Caught another Booby and prepared it for dinner with
7	5				the other Caught last Night. Served ½ lb Bread and a Gill of
8	5	4			Water for Breakfast
9	5				Many Birds Boobies and Noddies. —
10	5				
11	5				
12	5				Fine Wʳ but very hot. – People very faint – I divided the two Birds
	109				with all the offals and Fish and distributed the Shares with Bread
22	62				and Water as Yesterday
23	71		Merᵈ Altᵈ ☉ Center }	55..13°	

		Latitude		Longitude	
Course	Disᵗ	Obsᵈ	DR	DR	
N82 W	209	13..26 S	13..27 S	146..16 E	

The Weather is now serene, but unhappily we feel we are not able to bear the Suns heat, many of us suffering a languor and faintness which gives an indifference to life — We were however so fortunate to catch two Boobies to day their Stomachs contained several Flying Fish and Squids all of which I saved to be divided for dinner. —

We passed much drift Wood and saw many Birds. — I therefore did not hesitate to pronounce that we were near the Reefs of New Holland, and assured every one I would now without delay make the Coast in about the Parralell I was in and Range the Reef untill I found an opening through which we should get into Smooth Water and pick up some supplies — From my recollection of Capt. Cook's Survey of this Coast it considered the situation of it to be NW. and I was therefore satisfied that with the Wind to the Southward of East I could always clear any danger. — I found it also absolutely necessary to give a change to the miserable Situation some of my People were in. —

At Noon after writing up my Account I divided the two Birds with the entrails and contents of their Maws into 18 portions, and as the prize was a very valuable one it was divided as before by calling out who shall have this? — so that to day with with the allowance of 724 lb of Water at Breakfast and another at dinner with the proportion of Water. I was happy to see that every person thought he had feasted. ——

H	K	F	Courses	Winds	Rem^s Thursday 28th May 1789. Bountys Launch New Holland
1	5		West	E N E	Fresh Breezes and fine W^r with a fair going Sea.— Bailing every ten
2	5				Minutes keeps the Boat free of Water.—
3	4	6			
4	4	4			
5	4	6	..	..	Clouds keeping very fixed in the West leads me to believe we are
6	4	6			drawing near to New Holland.— Saw a Gannet
7	4		W½N		Served two Gills of Water only for Supper.
8	4				
9	4	4			
10	4	4		East	
11	4	4			
12	4	4		E S E	
1	4		..	..	Heard the sound of Breakers and saw them under our lee Bow bear^g
2	4		N N E.		W S W. about ¼ of a Mile. breaking very high— Hauled the Wind and
3	4				in 10 Minutes we could neither hear or See them.—
4	4				
5	4			S E	
6	4		..	..	Nothing in Sight I steered in again for the Coast.
7	3	4	W½N		
8	4				
9	3		..	..	Saw the Reef extend^g from N N W. to S B W. three miles off— hauled the Wind
10	2		N N E	E	At 9½ saw an opening and distant land like an Is^ld bear^g S W½N 7 or 8
	1	4	W½N		leag^s dis^t Bore away and entered a Safe Channel about 3 Cables length wide
11	5		W N W		with a strong Stream running in.—
12	4		N W		Untill 11 O'Clock tryed to keep hold of the Reef to Fish but could not on Acc^t
	97				of the tide, I therefore bore away at 11 O'Clock. the Channel I came in at E S E ½ Mile
23	71				At Noon. Fine W^r and smooth Water, the land first seen or Is^ld of Direction N N W.
24	60		Merid^n. Alt^d O Center } 55..43		5 leag^s and other land N N W W ½ W.— Sheltered from the Sea by the Reefs without us
					Served ¼ lb. Bread and a Gill of Water for dinner.—

| Course | Dist | Latitude | | Longitude | Rem^s |
		Obs^d	DR	DR	
N 6 W	80	12..46 S	12..52 S	145..02 E	The course & dist^t at 11 O'Clock is the back bear^g of the Channel having entered it at 10 O'Clock

I have already mentioned a Gannet. and the Clouds kept so fixed in the West. that I had no doubt of being near to New Holland. and every person after taking his Gill of Water for Supper began to please themselves on conversing on the probability of what they would find. — At one in the Morning the person at the Helm heard the Sound of Breakers and I no sooner lifted my head than I saw them close under our lee not more than ¼ Mile from us. I now hauled. the Wind to the NNE and in 10 Minutes we could not see or hear them. —

I have already mentioned my reason for making New Holland so far to the Southward, for I never doubted of numerous openings in the Reef through which I could have access to the shore, and knowing the inclination of the Coast to be to the NW. and the Wind mostly to the Southward of East, I could range such a barrier of Reefs untill I found a passage which now became absolutely necessary without a moments delay to search for supplies and get into smooth Water, the very Idea of which seemed only now to keep some of my Peoples spirits up. — The Joy therefore was great after we had got clear of the Breakers, to which we were much nearer than I thought it possible for us to be without knowing it. —

In the Morning at day light I bore away again for the Reefs and saw them by nine oClock — The Sea broke furiously over every part and I had no sooner got near to them, than the Wind came at East. and could only lie along the line of the breakers, within which we saw the Water so smooth that every person already anticipated the heart felt Satisfaction he would receive as soon as we could accomplish my intention. — But I now found that we were embayed, and I could not lie clear with my Sails such a heavy Sea setting in and the

Wind having backed against us, so that our Situation was now become dangerous. I expected but little from the Oars because we had no Strength to pull them, and it was becoming every minute more and more probable that I should be obliged to take the Reef, in case we could not pull off. — Even this I did not doubt of effecting with success, when happily we discovered a Break in the Reef about 1 Mile from us and at the same time an Island of a Moderate height could be seen in the same direction bearing W½N — I entered the passage, with a Strong Stream running to the Westward, and found it about two Cables length broad and every appearance of deep Water. —

On the outside the Reef inclined to the NE for a few Miles and from thence to the NW, and on the South side of the entrance it inclined to the SSW as far as I could see it, and I conjecture a Similar passage to this I have now entered lies between it and the Breakers I first discovered which are in lat° 13..14 S. 26 Miles South of this Channel, the situation of which is 12..51 S: and Longitude 145..10 East

I cannot recollect what Latitude Providence Channel lies in but I consider it to be very near to where we have come in. —

Being now happily within the Reefs and Smooth Water, I endeavoured to keep hold of the Reef to fish but the Tide set me to the NW. — I therefore bore away in that direction, and having promised to land on the first convenient Spot we could find, all our past hardships already seemed to be forgot. —

At Noon I had a good Observation from whence the forgoing situations may be considered to be determined with some exactness, and the Island first seen which I have called the Isl⁰ of Direction, in fair Weather will always show the Channel when bearing West. and may be seen as soon as the Reefs from a Ships Mast heads being in the Lat° of 12..51 S. — These however are marks too Small for a Ship to hit unless it can here after be known that passages are numerous along the Coast through the Reef, which I am inclined to think they are, in which case the risk is not so great if the Wind is not directly on the Coast

I now guessed at the North part of New Holland lying in about the latitude of 10..30 S° and that the direction of the Coast was to the NW if my recollection was right, about which I was pretty certain. We have therefore about 64 or 70 leagues of Coast to run past to search for refreshments. —

We now returned God thanks for his gracious protection and with much content took our miserable allowance of 1/24 lb of Bread and a Gill of Water for Dinner

H	K	F	Courses	Winds	Rem.ᵗ Friday 29ᵗʰ May 1789 In the Bounty's Launch, New Holland.
1	4		NW	E	Fine W.ʳ and smooth Water.
2	4	4	NWbW		
3	4	6	WNW	ESE	
4	2	4		~	Came to a Grapnel on the end of a Key to try for Fish. The Isl.ᵈ
5	4		WbN		Direction south 3 or 4 Leag.ˢ and an Island WbN. about 4 or 5
6					Miles where I determined if possible to spend the Night. —
7					At 5 O'Clock past a small Rocky Isle. close to the larger one where
8					I was bound, and on the NW. Side between it and the Main
9					I found a fine Sandy Point where I brought to a Grapnel and
10					landed. It was now a quarter past 5 O Clock
11					The Northernmost land which I called Fair Cape bore NWbN ½ N
12					7 Leagues and a point of the Main opposite to us from SWbS to NW ½ W
1					distant ¼ Mile. A small Islot. was on with the North Extreme.
2					another bore NbW 4 or 5 Leag.ˢ distant. — A remarkable Peaked Hill.
3					on the Main NbW ¾ W about 8 Miles and land as far as SbE. but
4					the Island of Direction was not in sight from this part of the Island.
5					Found Oysters and Periwinkles — One half slept on Shore but
6					could make no Fire. —
7					In the Morning. Employed gathering Oysters and others
8					getting the Boat in Order. Made a Fire by a small Magnifying
9					Glass I always carried about me. — Dug and found a fine Well
10					of Water. — Made a fine Stew of Oysters and issued to be mixed with
11					it an Allowance of Bread and some Pork, and at Noon I dis-
12					tributed to each person a Full pint. — Found three kinds of Berries
	20				of which we eat without any bad effects. — People very weak
24	60				and troubled with dreadfull Tenesemus. — Signs of Natives having
24	80				been here. — Island Woody — Many Doves and other Birds. —

		Latitude		Longitude
Course	Dis.ᵗ	Obs.⁰	DR	DR
N66W	10	12..39 S	12..39 S	144..44 E

Journal

Soon after I had got within the Keys the Coast began to show itself very distinctly with a variety of high and low Lands some parts of which were covered with Wood — In my way towards the Shore I fell in with a point of a Reef which is connected with that towards the Sea, and here I dropt a Grapnel and tryed to catch Fish but had no success — The Island Direction now bore South 3 or 4 leagues — Two Islands lay about 4 Miles to the NBN and appeared elligible for a resting place if nothing more, but on my approach to the first I found it nothing but a Heap of Stones and its size too inconsiderable to admit of Shelter for the Boat — I therefore proceeded to the Next which was close to it, (and next the Main,) where on the NW side I found a Bay and a fine Sandy point to land at. — Our distance was about ¼ of a Mile from a projecting part of the Main bearing from SWBS. to NNW ¾ W. — I now landed to examine if there were any signs of the Natives being near us, but altho' I discovered some old fire places I saw nothing to alarm me for our situation during the Night. — Every one was anxious to discover something to eat, and I soon heard that Oysters were found on the Rocks, for the Tide was out, but it was now nearly dark and only a few were gathered. — We were therefore to wait for the Morning to know how to proceed, and I consented that one half of us should sleep on Shore and the other in the Boat, but a great difficulty we had to surmount was to make a fire, which as we could not accomplish we took our rest for the Night which happily was Calm and undisturbed. —

The Dawn of Day brought greater strength and Spirits to us than I expected, for notwithstanding every one was very weak, Yet I saw strength remaining which I hoped would enable me to encounter the difficulties I had to undergo. —

As soon as I saw that no Natives were immediatly near us I sent out parties in search of Supplies while others were putting the Boat in Order that I might be ready to go to Sea in case any unforseen cause might make it necessary. — The first object of this necessary work that demanded refitting was the Rudder, one of the Gudgeons having come out in the course of the Night and was lost. – This if it had happened at Sea would most probably have been the Cause of our perishing, as the Management of the Boat would have been lost, at least not so nicely performed, as the very heavy Seas required. – I had often expressed my fears of this accident that we might be prepared for it, and had taken the precaution to have Grummets fixed on each Quarter for Oars, but even our utmost readyness in using them I fear would not have Saved us – it appears therefore a very providential Circumstance that it has happened at this place and in our power to remedy the defect; for by accident we found a large Staple which answered the purpose. –

The Parties were now returned highly rejoiced at having found plenty of Oysters and fresh Water. I also had made a fire by help of a small magnifying Glass that I always carried about me to read of the divisions of my Sextants, and what was still fortunate one of the Men among the few things he had thrown into the Boat and Saved, was a peice of Brimstone and a Tinder Box, so that I secured Fire in future. –

By the presence of Mind of one of my People he brought away a Copper Pot, it was by being in Possession of this Article that I was enabled to make a proper use of the supply we had found, and with a mixture of Bread and a little Pork I made a Stew that was eatable by People of more delicate appetities, of which each person received a full pint. – In the distribution of it the Voraciousness of some and the moderation of others was very discernable to me. – The Master began to be disatisfyed the first, because it was not made into a larger quantity by the addition of Water, and shewed a turbulent disposition untill I laid my commands on him to be Silent. –

The General complaints of disease were a dizziness of the head – great Weakness of the joints and violent Tenesmus, most of us having had no evacuation since we left the Ship – I had constantly a severe pain at the pit of my Stomach, but none of our complaints were alarming, on the contrary every one retained marks of Strength that with a mind possessed of any fortitude could bear more fatigue than I hoped we had to undergo in my route to Timor. —

As I would not allow any one to expose himself to the heat of the Sun it being near Noon, every one took his alottment of Earth shaded by the Bushes or a Tree for a short repose.

The Oysters we found grew so fast to the Rocks that it was with difficulty they could be broke off. and discovered it to be the most expeditious way at last to open them where they were. — They were very sizeable and well tasted and gave us great relief, but to add to this happy circumstance in a hollow of the land. where grew some Wire Grass which indicated a moist situation, on forcing a Stick about 3 feet into the ground, we found Water, and with little trouble dug a Well which produced us as much as we were in need of. — It was very good, but I could not determine if it was a Spring or not. — our wants made it not necessary to make the Well deep and it flowed as fast as we emptied it which with the soil being apparently too loose to contain Water from the Rains renders it probable to be a Spring. It lies about 200 Yards to the SE of Restoration point on the SW part of the Island. —

I found evident signs of the Natives resorting to this Island. for besides fire places I saw two Miserable Wigwams having only one side covered. We found a pointed Stick about three feet long. with a Slit in the end of it to Sling Stones with and is just the Same as the Natives of Van Diemens land use. — The Track of some Animal was very conspicuous on the Sand, and Mr Nelson agreed with me it was Kongoro, but how this Animal can get from the Main I know not, unless brought over by the Natives to breed. that they may take them with more ease, and render a Supply of food certain to them which on the Continent may be precarious and only to be got with great trouble owing to the extent of Country. — The Island may be about 2 Miles in extent, it is a high

Lumps of Rocks and Stones covered with Wood, but the Trees are small with only sufficient soil to produce them, which of itself is very indifferent and Sandy.— The Trees that came within our Knowledge were the Toa.— Manchineel and a species of the Burrow — also some Palm Trees the Tops of which we cut down, and the soft interior part or heart of them I found to be so palatable that I allowed it to be put into our Mess. — Mr. Nelson discovered some Fern Roots which I thought might be good roasted as a succedaneum for Bread. but it proved a very poor One., it however was very good in its Natural State to allay thirst, and I therefore directed a quantity to be collected to take into the Boat.— Many pieces of Cocoa Nutt shells and Husk were found about the Shore, but could find no Trees or did I see any like them on the Main.——

    Altho I had cautioned every one not to touch any kind of fruit that they might meet with, yet they were no sooner away than every one was secretly plucking of three different kinds that grew all over the Island, and eating without any reserve.— The Symptom only of having eaten too much began at last to frighten some of them, and on asking others who had taken a more moderate doze once found their minds a little quieted that no such complaint rested with them, but those became equally alarmed in their turn expecting that such symptoms would come on, and that they were all poisoned; so that they regarded each other with the Strongest marks of apprehension of what would be the issue of their imprudence.— Happily the Fruit proved wholesome and good. —— One kind grew on a Small delicate Vine. they were about the size of a Gooseberry and of a very like substance, but it had only a Sweet taste. the Skin was a pale red streaked with Yellow and was a pleasant Fruit. — Another kind grew on Bushes like what is called the Sea side Grape in the West Indies there were very like Elder Berries — The third was a black berry not so plenty as the others and not unlike a Bullum or large kind of Sloe both in size and taste — The seeing these fruit eat hollow by the Birds and insects led me to consider them fit for use, and those who had already tried the experiment properly finding no bad effects, made it a certainty that we might eat of them without fear.

Wild Pigeons, Parrots and other Birds were about the summit of the Island, but as I had no Fire Arms any relief of that kind was not to be expected unless I met with some unfrequented Spot where I might catch them with our hands. — This led me to a comparison of the vast difference in the sagacity of the feathered Species and Animals — Of the latter I know of no instance excepting the domesticated part, where they are not wiley and run from the approach of a human Being or make a prey of him, but the former on the contrary in unfrequented situations delight in the Novelty untill the feel the effect of the propensity that Man has to destroy them. — What is still remarkable that in ever so unfrequented a spot the land Birds are not so tame as the Sea. —

About a half Mile round on the South side of the Island from the Well, a small Run of Water was found, but as its source was not traced I know nothing more of it. —

The shore of this Island is very rocky except the part we were at, where on the Beach I picked up many pieces of Pumice Stone. — The part of the Main next to us had several sandy Beaches, but at low Water it had an extensive Rocky Flat. The Country had rather a barren appearance except in a few places where it was covered with Wood — A remarkable range of Rocks lay a few Miles to the S.W. and a high Peaked Hill terminated the Coast towards the Sea with other high Lands and Islands to the Southward. —

A high Fair Cape showed the direction of the Coast to the Southward about seven leagues and two Small Isles lay 3 and 4 leagues North of us. —

I saw a few Bees or Wasps — several Lizards, and the black Berry bushes were full of Ants Nests spun as spiders is but so close and compact as not to admit the Rain. —

A Trunk of a Tree about 50 feet long lay on the Beach from whence I conclude a heavy Sea runs in here in the time of the Northerly Winds

This being the Day of the Restoration of King Charles the Second, and the name being not inapplicable to my present situation for it has restored us to fresh life and strength) I named it Restoration Island, for I think it probable Capt. Cook may not have taken notice of it. The other Names I presume to give the different parts of the Coast are only to show my Route a little more distinct. —

Very fine Weather with ESE and SE Winds. —

This afternoon I sent the Parties out again to gather Oysters, and with some of the inner part of the Palm Top we got another good Stew made for Supper, of which I issued to each person a full pint and half, but I refused Bread to this Meal for I considered my wants might yet be very great, and as such I represented the necessity of saving our principal support whenever it was in our power. — This occasioned some murmuring with the Master and Carpenter, the former of whom wanted to prove a propriety of such an Expenditure, and was troublesomely ignorant tending to create disorder among those, if any were weak enough to listen to him. —

At Night I again divided, and one part slept in the Boat and the other by a good fire. — In the Morning I discovered a visible alteration in every one for the better, and I sent them away again to gather Oysters. — I had now only two lbs of Pork left and I promised to give it for dinner. — This Article which I could not keep under lock and key as I did the Bread. was exposed to the theft of some inconsiderate persons, but every one most sacredly denied it. I therefore resolved to put it out of their power for the future. — While the party was out Oystering I got the Boat in readyness for Sea, and filled all our Water Vessels which now amounted to nearly 60 Gallons. — The party being returned the Dinner was soon ready and every one had as good an Allowance as they had for Supper, for with the Pork I had given an allowance of Bread, and I was determined forthwith to push on. — As we had yet time before Noon I told every one that an exertion should now be made to gather as many Oysters as possible for a Sea Store as I was determined to sail in the Afternoon, but our full Bellies made us forget the Necessity and I had an opposition to such a plan Alledging they were too Weak. I was told also that when they were from me there were several complaining of my stay at this place and that it was much better to be going on, I that these unthankfull people were no sooner saved from perishing with want and fatigue than they had forgot the mercies they had received. I therefore after reprobating their conduct sent them out for a Sea Store and assured them they should now pursue their Voyage at all events gather what they would. —

About Noon they returned with the few Oysters they had time to pick up and every thing was put into the Boat. I also examined the quantity of Bread and I found 30 days allowance at my last mode of issuing 1/24 of a lb at Breakfast and 1/24 of a lb at Dinner. —

At Noon I had a good Observation for the latitude and found it to be 12°..39' S°. It was high Water at Noon and the Tide rose 3 feet. Flood from the Northward. — From this I deduce the time of high Water at full and change to be at 10 Minutes past 7 in the Morning. —

H	K	F	Courses	Winds	Rem.ˢ Sunday 31ˢᵗ May 1789 In the Bountys Launch, N. Holland
1	..	..		ESE	Very fine W.ʳ
2					
3			..	..	Performed prayers
4	..	..	..	..	Saw Natives on the Main. — Sailed strong Tide in our favor.
5	3	2	NBW		
6	3	2	..	..	Fair Cape NWBW ¾ W. 4 leag.ˢ A small Key NEBN 6 Miles. The
7	4		NW	SE	one seen from our landg place, NBW. 6 or 7 Miles. — Restoration Isl.ᵈ
8	3	4	NWBW		SSE ¼ E 7 Miles nearly on with Isl.ᵈ of Direction. the latter being only
9	3	4	WBW		just discernable. — Fair Cape being the Northernmost land in sight
10	3	4			
11	3	4	NBW		
12	2	6			
1	2	4	N.º		
2	2	6	..	..	Hauled the Wind as I found I was embayed. —
3	3	4	NE		K.º
4	3		I.º	ESE	
5	2	4			
6	2	6	..	..	K.º Fair Cape SSE 5 leagues East part of the Main N.º 4 Miles
7	3	4	NEBE	SEBE	Islands from N ¼ E 4 Miles to ESE 6 Miles Steered between them
8	2		N.º	..	and the Main where seven Natives came to the shore armed with
9					Spears and other Weapons. —
10					At 8 Ilanded on the largest and Northernmost of these Isles from
11					whence the Main low and sandy, bore WBN 3 leag.ˢ with two small
12					Keys off it. and the Southern part to be seen SⁱⁿE 4 Miles being Indian Bay
					Sent Parties out for Supplies. — I went on the heights to look at the Coast
	(10)				Saw it no farther. — A Key NWBN.
24	80				At Noon observed by the marks on the Rocks, that the Tide at times
25	36		Wind alt		rose 4 and 5 feet. —
			☉ Center } 56. 5		

Course	Dis.ᵗ	Obs.ᵈ	D.R	D.R
N 19 W	43	11.. 5 0 S	12.. 14 S	144.. 29 E

Journal Sunday 31st May 1789 – In the Bountys Launch, New Holland.

Being all ready for Sea. I directed every person to attend prayers, and by 4 O'Clock were preparing to embark, when we saw twenty Natives running and hollowing to us on the Opposite shore. – They were armed with a Spear or Lance, and a Shorter Weapon which they carried in their left hands, and made signs for us to come to them. – On the top of the Hill we saw the heads of many more, whether these were their Wives and Children or others who waited for our landing untill which they meant not to show themselves lest we might be intimidated, I cannot say, but as I found we were discovered to be on the Coast, I thought it prudent to make the best of my way for fear of Cannoes, altho from the accounts of Captn. Cook the chance was that there were very few or none of any consequence. – I passed these People as near as I could, which was within a quarter of a Mile, but I can only say that they were naked, and apparently black, and their Hair or Wool bushy and Short. –

I directed my Course for a Small Island bearing NBW from Restoration point, and from thence to Fair Cape, with a Strong Tide in my favor, so that I was abreast of it by 8 O'Clock. – The Coast I had passed was high and Woody, and to the SE of the Isle seen from Restoration point lay another, neither of which are worth Notice but as laying in the Way. – As I could see no land without Fair Cape I concluded that the Coast inclined to the NW. and NBW. and it was agreeable to my recollection of Captn. Cooks survey of it. I therefore steered acordingly, but by eleven oClock at Night I found myself mistaken as I met with low land, which inclined to the NE, so that 3 oClock in the Morning I was obliged to stand away to the Southward as I found I was embayed. –

At day break I was exceedingly surprized to find the appearance of the Country all changed, as if in the Course of the Night I had been transported to another part of the World, for I had now a miserable low Sandy Coast in view with very little Verdure, or any thing to indicate it was at all habitable to a human being, if I except some patches of small Trees or Brush Wood. —

I had many small Islands in View to the NE about 6 Miles distant. The East part of the Main bore North 4 Miles, and Fair Cape NbE 5 or 6 Leagues. — I took the channel between the nearest Island and the Main about 1 Mile apart, leaving all the Islands on the Starboard side. — Some of these were very pretty Spots covered with Wood and well situated for fishing. Large schools were about us but we could not catch any — As I was passing this Streight we saw another party of Indians seven in Number, running towards us shouting and making signs for us to land. Some of them waved green branches of the bushes that were near them as a token of friendship, but there were some of their other motions less friendly. A large party we saw coming, and I therefore determined not to land altho I wished much to have had some intercourse with these People, for which purpose I beckoned them to come near to me and laid the boat close to the Rocks, but not one would come within 200 Yards of us. — They were armed as those I had seen from Restoration Island. Stark naked, Short bushy Hair and in every respect the same people. —

An Island of a good height now bore N½W 4 Miles from us at which I resolved to see what could be got and from thence to take a look at the Coast, and here I landed about 8 OClock in the Morning. — The shore was rocky with some sandy Beaches within it, the Water however was smooth and I landed without any difficulty — I now sent two parties out one to the Northward and the other to the Southward to see what could be got, and others I ordered to stay by the Boat. — A muttering now began who had done the most, and some declared they would rather go without their Dinner than go out, In short I found I had but little Command among a few if they had not feared I was yet able to enforce it by more than laying simply my Commands. —

The Carpenter began to be insolent to a high degree, and at last told me with a mutinous aspect he was as good a Man as I was. — I did not just now see where this was to end, I therefore determined to strike a final blow at it, and either to preserve my Command or die in the attempt, and taking hold of a Cutlass I ordered the Rascal to take hold of another and defend himself, when he called out that I was going to kill him, and began to make concessions I was now only assisted by Mr. Nelson, and the Master very deliberately called out to the Boatswain to put me under an Arrest, and was stirring up a greater disturbance, when I declared if he interfered when I was in the execution of my duty to preserve Order and regularity, and that in consequence any tumult arose. I would certainly put him to death the first person. This had a proper effect on this Man, and he now assured me that on the contrary I might rely on him to support my Orders and directions for the future. This is the out lines of a tumult which lasted about a quarter of an hour. — I saw there was no carrying command with any certainty or Order but by power, for some had totally forgot every degree of obedience — I saw no one openly scouting the Offenders altho they were known, and I was told that the Master and Carpenter at the last place were endeavouring to produce altercations and were the principal Cause of the murmuring there. — Such is generally the case under such disastrous circumstances as mine. I now took a Cutlass determined never to have it from under my Seat, or out of my Reach, as providence had seemed pleased to give me sufficient strength to make use of it, it   I did not suffer this to interfere with the harmony of the well disposed who it is my duty to make known, — They were Mr. Nelson. Mr. Samuel. Mr. Hayward. Mr. Peckover Mr. Ledward. Mr. Elphinstone Mr. Hallett. Mr. Cole. John Smith and Lawce Lebogue. — and I ordered the parties to go on to collect what could be found, which consisted of some fine Oysters and Clams, and a few Small Dog Fish were Caught in the Holes of the Rocks. — We also found about Two Ton of Rain Water in a hollow of the Rocks on the North part of the Island, so that of this essential article we were again so happy as not to be in want. —

After regulating the mode of proceeding I set off to the highest part of the Island to see and consider of my route for the Night. — To my surprize I could see no more of the Main than I did below, it extending only from S½ E 4 Miles to WBN about 3 leagues full of Sand Hills. — Besides the Isles to ESE and So that I had seen before I could only discover a small Key in the NWBN — As this was considerably farther from the Main than where I was at present, I resolved to get there by Night it being a more secure resting place, for I was here open to an Attack of the Indians had Cannoes, as they undoubtedly observed my landing — My mind being made up in this point I returned taking a particular look at the Spot I was on, which I found only to produce a few tropical Bushes and Coarse Grass, and the extent of the whole not more than 2 Miles in Circuit. — On the North side in a Sandy Bay we found an old Cannoe about 33 feet long bottom up and half burried in the Beach — It was made of three peices — the bottom entire to which the sides were sewed in a common way — It had a sharp projecting prow rudely carv'd in resemblance of a Fishes head. — The extreme breadth was about 3 feet and I imagine it was capable of carrying twenty Men. — I now returned and Observed the Latitude.

The parties were all in, but found difficulty in gathering the Oysters from their adhering so close to the Rocks and the Clams were not plenty. — I therefore saw that without delaying time for a day or two and not even then I should be able to collect but few more than we could eat, for as real and actual exertions were wanting any tolerable Sea Store could not be expected unless I fell in with a greater plenty. —

H	K	F	Courses	Winds	Rem.ᵗˢ Monday 1ˢᵗ June 1789. In the Bountys Launch. New Holland.
1				WBS	Very fine Wᵉ and Smooth Water. —
2					Dined on a plentifull Meal of Stewed Oysters, and Clams, and Sailed
3					at 3 o'Clock – called this Island. Sunday after the Name of the day. —
4	4	6	NWBN		
5	4	6	..	..	A high peaked Mountain opened with the south part of the Main at
6	4	6			WBS ¾ S and could see the Coast as far as WNW. with white Sand Hills very
7					conspicuous —
8					At 6 o'Clock I arrived at the Key I intended to spend the Night at
9					but the tide being low. and a very rocky Shore, I could not land
10					without risk of getting some of the Rocks through the Boats bottom
11					I therefore brought to a Grapnel for the Night. —
12					
1					
2					
3					
4					
5					
6	.		~	..	At day light got the Boat in upon the Beach – Saw a Turtle
7					Track – sent parties off to see what they could pick up. —
8					
9					People complaining of Sickness at the Stomach and dreadfull
10					Tenesmus. —
11					
12	-	-	..	SE.	A very fresh Gale and fair Wʳ. Parties returned with some Clams
14					Mr Nelson Ill. —
2536			Merid.ʳ Alt.ᵈ		
2550			ʘ Center	56..09	

Course	Dist	Latitude		Longitude	Rem.ᵈ
		Obs.ᵈ	DR	DR	Low Water at Noon. —
NNW	12	11..47 S	11..47 S	144..24 E	

At 2 o'Clock this afternoon I issued to every one a full pint and a half of Stewed Oysters and Clams which I had thickened with a small Bean which Mr. Nelson informed me was species of Dollichus, and having dined heartily and taken what Water we were in Want of, I only waited to determine high Water which I found to be at 3 o'clock and the rise of the Tide about 5 feet. — According to this it is high Water at full and Change at 19 Min.s past 9 in the Morning, but here I observed the Flood to come from the Southward altho at Restoration Island I thought it came from the Northward, so that there appears an error in the latter if we take the Tide flowing later here as a criterion to judge from. — but I think Capt.n Cook speaks of great irregularity with respect to the set of the Flood as he found it on this Coast. —

I now Sailed for the Key I had seen in the NWBN, giving the name of Sunday Island to the Place I had left. — I got to it just at dark, but found it so surrounded by a Reef of Rocks that I could not land without a risk of Staving the Boat and therefore I came to a Grapnel for the Night. —

At Dawn of Day we got on shore and tracked the Boat into shelter, for the Wind blowing fresh without and the Ground rocky, I was affraid to trust her at a Grapnel lest she might be blown to Sea. I was on this Account reduced to the Necessity to let her ground in the course of the Ebb. — From appearances I expected in the Course of the following Night to meet with Turtle as we had already discovered recent tracks of them. — innumerable Birds of the Noddy kind made it likewise their resting place; so that upon the Whole I flattered myself of getting supplies in greater abundance than it had hitherto been in my power The Situation was 4 leagues from the Main, and we were on the N Westermost of four small Keys which surrounded by a Reef of Rocks connected by Sand Banks; except between the two Northermost where it was only passable at low Water over Rocks formed a Lagoon Island into which the Tides flowed, and where at the entrance I kept the Boat. —

As usual I sent Parties away in search of

supplies, but to my astonishment we could only get a few Clams and some Dolichus with these and the Oysters. We had brought from Sunday Island, I made up a Mess for Dinner with an addition of a small quantity of Bread. —

Towards Noon Mr. Nelson and his party who had been to the Eastward They returned but himself in such a weak condition that he was obliged to be supported by two Men. — His complaint was a burning in his Bowels a loss of sight, much drought and an incapacity to walk. — This I found was owing to his not being able to support the heat of the Sun, and that being fatigued and faint instead of getting into the Shade he had continued to do more than he was able. — It was a great happiness to me to see on their calling me in that he had no Fever, and it was now my Medicine the little Wine that I had carefully saved became of real use. — I gave it him in very small quantities with some small pieces of Bread soaked in it, and having pulled of his Cloaths and laid him under some Shady Bushes he began to get better. — The Boatswain and Carpenter also became ill and complained of Head ach and Sickness of the Stomach. — Others who had not had any evacuation by Stool became shockingly distressed with the Tenesmus, so that I had but few who were not complaining. —

Some one now mentioned that he thought their illness was occasioned by eating the Dollichus, when it spread like Wild fire, and those who were complaining thought themselves poisoned. — Myself however and some others who had eat of them were yet very well but the truth was, all those except Mr. Nelson. who were complaining had gorged themselves with a large quantity of undressed Beans, and Mr. Nelson informed me that they were constantly teazing him whenever a Berry was found if it was good to eat, so that it would not surprize him if many of them were realy poisoned. —

Our Dinner was not so well relished as at Sunday Island because we had mixed the Dollichus with the Stew — Oysters and Soup however was eat by every one except Mr. Nelson, who eat only a few small pieces of Bread soaked in a small Glass of Wine and began to recover. —

In my walk round the Island I found several Cocoa Nutt Shells. — the remains of an Old Wigwam and two backs of Turtle, but no sign of any Quadruped — One of my People found three Fowls Eggs. —

As is common on such Spots, the Soil is little other than Sand, Yet it produced small Toa Trees and several others we were not acquainted with— There were Fish in the Lagoon, but we could not catch any, as our wants therefore were not likely to be supplied, not even Water for our daily expence, I told every one I would Sail in the Morning after trying our success in the Night for Turtle and Birds — A quiet Night to rest. I also conceived would be of essential Service to those who were unwell. —

From the Wigwam and Turtle Shell being found. it is certain that the Natives resort to this place at certain times of the Year, and it likewise proves beyond a doubt of their having Cannoes — it did not appear to me I was running any risk by remaining here, and I directed our Fire to be made among the thicket that we might not be discovered in the Night. —

The Main extended as far as N.W. full of white Sand Hills and a Small Island lay W.b.N ¾ N 3 leagues from us - My situation being very low. I could see nothing of the Reef towards the Sea. —

HKF	Courses	Winds	Rem.ˢ Tuesday 2.ⁿᵈ June 1789. In the Bountys Launch. New Holland.
1	..	SE	Strong Gales and Squally W.ʳ some slight showers.
2			
3			
4	..	..	Boiled some Clams for to Morrows dinner and cut the rest up in
5			slices for to dry — High Water at 5..30 — Full and Change 50 past
6			10 in the Morning. — Gave People who were unwell a little bread &
7			Wine and I was happy to find them much better. —
8	.. ..	..	.. Parties now went out to look for Turtle and Catch Birds. —
9			
10			
11			
12	.. ..	..	.. The Bird party returned with only 12 Small Birds owing to
1			the fault of One of the Men going too hastily among them —
2			
3	.. ..	..	.. M.ʳ Samuel and M.ʳ Peckover returned from searching
4			after Turtle but did not get a Sight of one. —
5			
6	..	..	Sailed with a Strong Breeze.
7	4 6	NbW	.. Came into much Sea as if here was no shelter from Reefs with-
8	5	NbW	out. — Passed an extensive Shoal and two Sandy Spots on it. —
9	5		At 8 a Small Isle N ½ E 3 or 4 leag.ˢ two others West about 4 Miles. —
10	5		Apparently smoother and deeper Water in Shore.
11	5	..	.. A Sandy Key East 3 Miles. —
12	4 4	..	.. Fresh Breezes and fair W.ʳ a Small Isl.ᵈ NE 2 Miles. a Sandy Spit ENE
29			3 Miles. an Isl.ᵈ beyond it EbN ½ N. 6 Miles and the N.West.ᵈ Land seen
2550			from Lagoon Isl.ᵈ and is a high Cape W ¾ S 3 leag.ˢ A low Sandy Isle
2579			West 4 Miles and the extremes of the Coast from SbW to NN ½ N
			Dined on 6 Birds and an Allowance of Bread with 2 Gills Water. —

			Latitude		Longitude
Courses	Dis.ᵗ	Obs.ᵈ	DR	DR	
N ½ W	30	11..10..S	11..17 S	144..20 E	

Rest was now so much wanted that the afternoon was advantageously spent in sleep, I had however some who were not disposed to it, and with those I employed myself in dressing some Clams to take with us for to morrows dinner, and others I had cut up in slices to dry which I knew and foretold was the most valuable Supply I could find. — But contrary to my expectation we have found them very scarce, and I do not, from the present situation we are in, imagine I shall be able to get collected two days Sea Store at a very Spare allowance. —

Towards Evening I had cautioned every one not to make too large a Fire or to suffer it after dark to blaze up more than it was possible to prevent — Mr. Peckover and Mr. Samuel had therefore taken care of that business while I was strolling about the Beach to observe if I thought it could bee seen from the Main — I was just reconciled that it could not when on a sudden the Key appeared all on a blaze that might have been seen at a more considerable distance. — I therefore ran to know the Cause of such an Open Violation of my orders when I found all the Grass set on fire owing to the Master while I was absent insisting on having a fire to himself, notwithstanding Mr. Peckover an Samuel had remonstrated with him and told him the Consequence, and he knew very particular orders. This disobedience was of a very serious nature I might have been seen by more Natives than at the last place, as I past the Coast, and now being assured that we were on this Key it only rested with them to come after us. and we must inevitably have fallen a sacrifice, for even when all were in health I had only 12 Men that had either Spirit or resolution to Combat any difficulty. — Thus the relief I expected from a little Sleep was totally lost, and I anxiously looked for the flowing of the Tide to proceed to Sea. —

I found it High Water at half past 5 this Morning from whence I fix its time on full and Change to be at 58 past 10 in the Morning and I imagine the rise to be about 5 feet. — I could observe nothing of the Flood, but I presume it comes from the Southward, and that I may have been mistaken at Restoration Island, for I draw my conclusion from the times of High Water, and my observation at Sunday Island Viz.ᵗ —

At Restoration Island. High Water full and Change . . . . . . 7ʰ 10′

Sunday - Is.ᵈ — flood from South.ᵈ . . . . 9 . 19

Here . . . . 10 . 50.

After 8 O Clock M.ʳ Samuel and M.ʳ Peckover went out to watch for Turtle and three men went to the East Key to endeavour to take some Birds all the rest complaining of being Sick, took their rest except M.ʳ Hayward and M.ʳ Elphinstone who I ordered to keep Watch. — About Midnight the Bird party returned with only 12 Noddies a Bird I have already described to be about the size of a small Pigeon, but if it had not been for the obstinacy of one of the Party, who seperating from the other two and putting the Birds to flight, they might have caught a great Number, thus all my Plans were totally defeated for which on the return of the offender I gave him a good beating. — I now went in search of my Turtling party who had taken every pains but had met with no success - this however did not surprize me, as I was convinced no Turtle would come near us after the fire and Noise that was made in the beginning of the Evening to get it put out. — I therefore desired them to come in, but they requested to stay an hour or two longer as they still hoped to find some before day light, they however returned by 3 OClk without any reward for their labour. —

The Birds I got half dirst, which with a few Clams made the whole of my supply here. — I tied up a few Gilt Buttons and some pieces of Iron to a Tree for any Natives that might come after me, and happily finding my Invalids much better for their Nights rest. I got every one into the Boat and departed at Dawn of Day. Wind at S.E Course to the N.b.W.

I had scarce got two leagues to the Northward when I suddenly fell into much Sea, which from not having experienced such a sudden transition since within the Reefs I considered it owing to an open Channel to the Ocean. — Just afterwards I fell in with a large Shoal on which were two Sandy Keys, between these and two others 4 Miles West I passed on in my way to the Northward crossing a rougher Sea than I had before.   Towards Noon I fell in with 6 other Keys most of them produced some small Trees and Brush Wood, and it had a pleasing contrast with the Main Shoal, passed which was full of Sand Hills — The Country now became Hilly and the Northernmost Land, the same as I saw from Lagoon Island appeared as Downs with several sloping Clifts to the Sea. To the South.ᵈ of this is a flat Top'd Hill resembling a Pudding Pan turned bottom up and was called Pudding Pan Hill and a little to the Northward two others called the Paps and here was a small tract of Country without Sand. the Eastern part of which forms a Cape that I consider to lie in Lat.ᵈ of 16..10 S. From hence the Coast inclines to the N W B N. — At Noon I observed in the Lat.ᵈ of the Cape 16..10 S.ᵗ — Five small Keys lie from the N E to the S E from 2 to 6 Miles distant and one to the West — between me and the Cape a low Sandy Spot bearing West distant 4 Miles — My Long.ᵈ 144..20 East and N N W dist.ᵗ 30 Miles from Lagoon Island. — I am sorry it is not in my power to speak of the depth of Water, that would create trouble and delay, but as every other remark & observation that can be made falls upon myself, I can only say that a Ship may pass wherever I omit representing danger, as far as a Mans judgement can be relied on that is formed from appearances. —

        I divided 6 Birds and issued 124 lb of Bread and 2 Gills of Water to each person for dinner, and to Mr. Nelson I gave a half Glass of Wine who is now so far recovered as to require no other indulgence. — The Gunner when he left the Ship brought his Watch with him and had regulated our time untill to day when unfortunately I found it stopt. so that at Noon. Sun Rise and Set are the only parts of the 24 Hours I can speak to particularly as to time. —

H	K	F	Courses	Winds	Rem.s Wednesday 3.d June 1789. Bounty's Launch. New Holland
1	4	4	N.B.W	S.E.B.S.	Fresh Breezes and fair W.r
2	5	4			
3	4	4			
4	5		N.W.		The Cape I was abreast of at Noon now bore true South 6 or 7 Leagues
5	5				and the farthest part of the Coast to the North N.W.B.W. low land with
6	4			S.S.E	hillocks. — At 5.h an Inlet bore S.W.B.S. 6 Miles. —
7					At 5.h 3/4 came to a Grapnel off an Island 6 Miles from the Main. — The
8	-		Fresh Gales		extremes of the Main bore from N.N.W.1/2 W. 3 Leagues. to S.E.B.S. 6 or 7 Leagues
9					A Mountainous Isl.d with a flat Top N.B.W. 4 or 5 Leag.t and several others
10					between it and the Main. —
11					Parties went out in search of Supplies found nothing but the remain
12					of many Turtle that have been killed here. —
1					
2					
3					
4					
5					At 1/2 past 4 Sailed with a fresh Gale.
6	2		N.B.W.	S.E.B.S.	Serv.d 1/24 lb. Bread. and a Gill of Water for breakfast. —
7	5				
8	5		N.N.W.		Passing between Mountain Isl.d with a flat Top, and several others towards
9	5		N.W.B.W.	S.E.B.S.	the Main dist.t across 3 Miles. Sounded 12 f.m.s
10	5	2			Passed a Bay of Isl.ds, and others to the East.d — an Isl.d in the North very
11	5	4	N.W.	S.E.B.S.	Mountainous with a very high round Hill and continued passing
					others both to the North and South
12	4		S.W.	S.S.E	At Noon fresh Breezes and fair W.r — The Main high and Woody.
	1	4			Wednesday Island E.B.S. 5 Miles. Isles on the North from N.W.B.W. 4 or 5 Leag.t
	63				to N.E. 6 Leag.t and the West extreme of the Coast S.W. 2 or 3 Leag.t — A
2	579				Reef from W. to N.E. one Mile off. —
2642			Merid.n Alt.d		
			☉ Center	57..07	

		Latitude		Longitude
Course	Dist	Obs.d	D.R	D.R
N.34.W	58	10..31 S	10..30 S	143..45 E

Journal

As I stood to the N.b.W. this Afternoon I found more Sea than I had done before, and of Course considered it owing to less shelter from the Reefs to the Eastward, or that perhaps there were none — at any Rate I concluded here is not one continued barrier to prevent shipping having access to the shore — I observed I was in a Stream setting to the N.W. which I considered to be the Flood, and I saw in some places along the Coast patches of Wood. —

At 5 OClock after steering to the N.W. I passed a large and fair Inlet, into which I imagine is a safe and commodious entrance, it lies in latitude of 11.00 about 3 leag.ts to the Southward of an Island the only one near it. — At this Island about a quarter before 6 OClock I took shelter for the Night under a Sandy Point which was the only part we could land at. — I was therefore under the necessity to put up with rather a Wild Situation and slept on the Boat Neverthelep I sent a Party away to see what could be got, but They returned without any Success — They saw a great number of Turtle Bones and Shells where the Natives had been feasting, and their last visit seemed to be of no late date. — The Isle was covered with Wood but in other respects a lump of Rocks. — I lay at a Grapnel untill day light with a very fresh Gale and Cloudy W.r The Main bore from N.N.W.½ W. 3 leag.ts to S.E.b.S 6 or 7 leagues. — A Mountainous Island with a Flat top N.b.W. 4 or 5 leagues and several others between it and the Main The Spot I am on which I call Turtle Island lies in lat.de by Account 10.° 52′ S and 42 Miles Westward of Restoration Island. — Abreast of it the Coast appears as a Sandy Desert, but improves again about 3 leag.ts farther to the Northw.d — Where it terminates to the N.E. in lat.de 10.° 45′ S.o with a Number of Islands. — I sailed between these Islands with no Ground at 12 fm.s The high Mountainous Island with a Flat Top. and four Rocks to the S.E of it, that I call the Brothers, on my Starboard hand. — Soon after an extensive opening in the S.W. appeared with a number of high Islands in it which I called the Bay of Islands — I crossed this Bay steering to the N.W. several Isles & Keys lay to the Northward taking the direction of the Coast. — The most northerly Island was Mountainous having a very high and remarkable Round Hill and a smaller Island to the SE was remarkable for a Single Peaked Hill. —

The Coast to the Northward and Westward of the Bay of Islands had a very different look. from that to the Southward. — It was high and Woody. with Islands more considerable than I had seen before and had a very broken Appearance. — Among these Islands are fine Bays and convenient places for Shipping. — The Northernmost I call Wednesday Island from whence to the NW. I fell in with a large Reef. which I believe joins a Number of Keys from the SW. to the NE. and ENE. I now stood to the SW. 1½ Mile when it was Noon. and I had a Good Observation and Wednesday Island bore EBS 5 Miles. — The Westernmost land. SW 2 or 3 leag.ˢ and the Islands to the Northward. from NWBW. 4 or 5 leagues to NE 6 leag.ᵗ The Reef from W. to NE dist.ᵗ one Mile — I now assured every one of being clear of New Holland in the Afternoon. —

It is impossible for me to say how far the Reef I fell in with may extend. — it may be a continuation or a detatched part. of the Range of Shoals that surround the Whole Coast, but be that as it may I. consider the Mountainous Islands as seperate from these Shoals. and towards those Isles whatever passages for Shipping there are I have no doubt that these will be found the best. But I recommend it to every person. who is to pass this Streight from the Eastward to take their direction from the. Coast of New Guinea, but I likewise think that a Ship coming from the Southward will find a fair Streight in the latitude of 10. 00 S. —

In the deplorable Situation I was in I would have endeavored. to have determined this point if I had. had any fire

Arms, but any encrease of trouble or fatigue I feared would have been of too dangerous a tendency. I therefore declared my intention of passing on without delay — Sounding as I have already remarked would have been a most satisfactory part of information yet I was obliged to lay it aside, but the labours that have rested with myself will I hope be of some use and give some new Ideas respecting this Streight. —

As an addition to ½ lb of Bread and a Gill of Water for Dinner I gave to each person 16 Oysters and for their Breakfast I could only afford them Bread and Water. —

H	K	F	Courses	Winds	Rem.[s] Thursday 4.th June 1789. Bounty's Launch New Holland
1	3		W.S.W.	S.E.	Fair W.r — Dined on 6 Oysters each person ½4 lb Bread & a Gill of Water.
2	3		..	..	At 2 Came into Shoal Water. and saw Sand banks lying to the North.d
3	3	4			of the West part of the Main. —
4	3	4	"	..	The Westm.t Isle North 4 leag.s. a Key West. Extremes of the land from Wednesd.y
5	4	4			Isle E.b.N 5 to S.E.b.E 2 leagues Shoal Cape. —
6	4	4			At ½ past 5 at Booby Key a barren Rock. The Main bore E.S.E to E.b.N.
7	4	6			Served Water for Supper. —
8	4	6			I steered different Courses between Noon and 4 O Clock, but I have only
9	4	6			inserted a Mean one computed by my bearings. —
10	5		..	..	Fresh Gale. —
11	5				I consider Booby Key to be the same as seen by Capt.n
12	5				Cook when he quitted the Coast —
1	5	6			
2	5	2			
3	4	6			
4	4	4			
5	5	2			
6	5	4	..	..	A cross going Sea. — Deep Water. — Very Wet and bailing Served ½4
7	5				lb Bread. and a Gill of Water for Breakfast. —
8	4	4			
9	5				
10	5				
11	5				
12	4	6	..	~	Fresh Breezes and fair W.r dined on 6 Oysters each person ½4 lb of
	113				Bread. and 2 Gills of Water —
	264 2				
	27 5 5		Mean Allo.w B Center }	5.° 43	

Course	Dist	Latitude		Longitude
		Obs.d	DR	DR
N 49 W	111	10.° 48 S	10.° 58 S	141.° 54 E

Journal

At 2 o'Clock as I was steering to the SW. towards the Westernmost part of the South Shore, I fell into Shoal Water occasioned by some large Sand Banks that lie there connected with the Coast. — I was therefore obliged to steer to the Northward again, and having got round them I directed my Course to the West. — At 4 o'Clock the Western.t Isle bore North 4 leagues. Wednesday Island. EBN 5 leagues and Shoal Cape SEBE 2 leagues. — A small Key was now seen bearing West, at which I arrived by dusk of the Evening, and found it a mere Rock, a place where Boobies resort to, and for this reason called it Booby Key. — A small Key also lies close to the West part of the Coast which I have called Shoal Cape. — Here terminated the Rocks and Shoals of the North part of New Holland. for I could see no land to the Westw.d of South after 3 o'Clock. — I am positive that Booby Key was seen by Capt.r Cook, but I cannot reconcile to myself the situation of any other part I have seen to my Idea of his Survey of the Coast unless Shoal Cape is his point possession. —

At 8 o'Clock in the Evening I was once again launched into the midst of an Open Ocean miserable as we were in every respect. — On reflection I was surprized to see it did not appear to effect any one as a melancholy matter of necessity; on the contrary it seemed as if every one had only embarked with me to proceed to Timor, and were in a Vessel equally calculated for their Safety and convenience. — So much confidence gave me great pleasure, & I may assert that owing to it we may attribute their being so well as they are, for whoever had despaired would have been dead before I got to New Holland. — I now gave every one hopes that eight or ten days might restore us to a land of Safety, and after praying to God for a continuance of his most gracious protection I served an Allowance of Water for Supper and kept my Course to the WSW. to counteract a Gale from the Southward. in case it should Overblow. —

I have been just six days on the Coast of New Holland, in the Course of which it is to be Observed. Oysters with a few Clams have been the only supply we met with besides Water. — Indeed it was all I could expect, but equal to this perhaps we have benefited by having no fatigue in the Boat and good rest at Night. — With these advantages every one has certainly prolonged his life, and poor as the Supply has been I am very sensible of the great good it has done, and has relieved my mind from many a distressing thought. — It would have been about this time that human Nature would have no longer been able to defend itself against hunger and extreme fatigue, several would have given up struggling with life that only insured wretchedness and misery, and those possessed of more bodily strength would on such a Sight soon have followed their miserable and unfortunate companions. — Even in our present situation we are reduced beings horrible to behold. Yet while any fortitude and Spirit remain we drag on, and I hope that the Idea of the End of our Misery being so near at hand will yet enable me to land every one safe at Timor —

For my own part wonderfull is it for me to relate, I feel no extreme hunger or thirst — My allowance satisfies me. knowing I can have no more. — This perhaps does not admitt me to be a proper judge on a story of miserable people like us being at last drove to the necessity of destroying one another for food, but if I may be allowed, I deny the fact in its greatest extent. — I say I do not believe that among us such a thing could happen, but death through famine would be received as from any violent disease. —

Served 6 Oysters and ¼ lb Bread. for dinner. —

H	K	F	Courses	Winds	Rem^s Friday 5th June 1789. Bounty's Launch towards Timor
1	4	4	W½S	ES.E.	Fair W^r and less Sea.
2	4	4			
3	4	6	,,	,,	Saw several small Water Snakes. Ringed Yellow and Black.—
4	3	4			
5	3	6			
6	3	4	,,	,,	Servd a Gill of Water for Supper.— I was asked for Bread but I
7	4				was not far enough advanced to judge of my passage to grant it.
8	4				At which there were some Murmurings by the Master & Carpenter
9	4				Simpson and Lintslitter —
10	4				
11	4				
12	4		,,	,,	Showers of Rain
1	4	4			
2	4	4			
3	4	4			
4	4	4			
5	4	4			
6	4	6	,,	,,	Fair W^r and a Strong Trade.— Constantly bailing.—
7	5				
8	5				
9	5		,,	,,	Saw Water Snakes, Rock Weed and flying fish.—
10	5		N	EBN.	
11	5	4			
12	5	4	,,	,,	D^o W^r Servd 1/24 lb Bread. and a Gill of Water for Dinner with
	100				6 Oysters to each person
	27	5			
	20	63	Merid^n Alt^d ʘ	} 56..40	
			ʘ Centre		

			Latitude		Longitude
Course	Dist^e	Obs^d	DR	DR
W¼N	100	10..45 S	10..43 S	140..04 E

Journal

In addition to our Allowance of 1/4 lb Bread. and a Gill of Water for breakfast and Dinner I served. 6 Oysters to each person —

We passed a Number of Water Snakes that were Ringed Yellow and black, and towards Noon a good deal of Reck Weed. — Altho the Weather is fair yet we are constantly wet with the Sea. and two people are always obliged to bail the Boat. —

H	K	F	Courses	Winds	REM.ⁿ Saturday 6ᵗʰ June 1789. Bountys Launch towards Timor
1	4	5	WBN.	EBS	Fine W.ʳ and a Strong Trade. constantly bailing
2	4	5			
3	4	5			
4	4	6			
5	5	4			
6	5	4	..	..	Caught a Booby. Divided the blood between three who were most in
7	5				Want. — Serve'd a Gill of Water and I directed the Bird to be kept for
8	5				Dinner
9	5	.			Constantly Shipping Water and Bailing —
10	5				
11	5				
12	5				
1	5				
2	5				
3	5				
4	5		..	SE	
5	5		..	..	Cloudy and showers — Very Cold and Shiverings — Found some of the Clams
6	5				I had hung up to dry for Sea store Stolen but every one sacredly denied
7	5				it. — Serve'd 1/24 lb Bread and Water for Breakfast. —
8	5				Saw a Sand Lark — Gannet — Water Snakes. —
9	5				
10	4	4			
11	4	4			
12	5	..	..	ESE	Cloudy with Fair Intervals. — I cut the Bird up in 18 parts and
	119				divided it according to the usual way of "who shall have this"?
	2)63				I gave 1/24 lb. of Bread. also and a Gill of Water. —
	3)32	Merid.ⁿ Alt.º	° ′		
		⊙ Center }	57..00		

			Latitude		Longitude
Course	Dist	Obs.ᵈ	DR	DR
N77ºW	117	10..19 S	10..11 S	138º..00 E

Journal

Constantly shipping Water and bailing — In the Evening a few Boobies came about us one of which I caught with my hand the blood was divided among three who were most in Want, but the Bird I ordered to be kept for dinner. Served a Gill of Water for Supper and two to those who chose it —

In the Course of the Night we suffered much Cold and Shiverings. — At day light I found some of the Clams I had hung up to dry for Sea store, taken away; but every one most sacredly denied it. — Saw a Gannet — a Sand Lark and some Water Snakes. — Served 1/24 lb Bread and Water for Breakfast and the same at dinner with the Bird which I issued according to the Usual way of "Who shall have this; — I determined to make Timor in the Lat.d of 9..30 or 10..00 South. —

H	K	F	Courses	Winds	Rem.ˢ Sunday 7ᵗʰ June 1789. Bounty Launch. Towards Timor
1	4	2	W.N.W.	E.s.E.	Fresh Breezes and fair Wᵣ. This afternoon examined my Store of
2	3	6	N.W.½.W.		Bread. and found 19 days allowance. according to my former issues
3	3	6	"		of ½ 4 lb three times a day to each person. — I therefore told every one that
4	3	6			they should now have their allowance as usual for Supper. —
5	3	6			
6	4		"		
7	4	3			
8	5		N.W.	S.E.	Fresh Gale constantly bailing. —
9	5	2			
10	5	2	"	"	Much Sea.
11	5				
12	5		"		
1	5	2			
2	5	2	N.W.½.W.		
3	5				
4	5		"	"	Cold and Wet
5	5				
6	5		"	"	Heavy Complaints of distress
7	5		W.N.W.	E.s.E	
8	5		"	"	Served ½ 4 lb Bread and Water for Breakfast. —
9	5		W.½.S		Many Tropic Gulls — Shearwaters and flying fish. —
10	4	4			
11	5				
12	4	4	"	"	Fresh Gales and Squally with much Sea from the N.E. —

111

29.42

30.9.3 Merid.ⁿ Alt.ᵈ ☉ Center } 57..42

Served ½ 4 lb Bread and Water for Dinner and Clams.

Steered W.N.W. to prevent us from Shipping so much Sea.

			Latitude		Longitude
Course	Dist	Obs.ᵈ	D.R.		D.R.
N.57.W	88	9..31 S	9..16 S		136..53 E

Journal

Constantly Wet and Bailing — In the Afternoon I took the opportunity of examining again my Store of Bread, and I found I had 19 days allowance at my former Rate of issuing 1/24 lb three times a day — I therefore now saw I had every prospect of making my passage in Time and granted an allowance for Supper. —

We passed the Night miserably Wet and Cold, and in the Morning I heard heavy complaints at our deplorable Situation — The Sea was high and breaking over us. — I could only afford the allowance of Bread and Water for Breakfast but for Dinner I gave about an Oz of dryed Clams to each person which was all that remained. — At Noon I altered my Course to the WNW to keep more from the Sea while it blows so Strong. —

H	K	F	Courses	Winds	Remks. Monday 8th June 1789. Bountys Launch Towards Timor
1	5	..	WNW	East	Fresh Gales and Squally with much Sea — Ship a great deal of
2	5				Water and are constantly Wet and Bailing: — I see with much
3	5				concern the Surgeon Mr. Ledward, and Lawrence Lebogue an Old
4	5				Hardy Seaman giving way very fast.
5	5				
6	5				Served 1/24 lb Bread, and Water for Supper. —
7	4				
8	4				
9	4				
10	4				
11	4				
12	4			EdS	
1	5	3			
2	5				
3	4	4		East	
4	5				
5	4	4			
6	4	4		EdS	Very Wet and Cold Gave a little Wine to the Surgeon & Lebogue.
7	4				
8	4			ENE	Squally with showers — Served 1/24 lb Bread and a Jill of Water
9	3	4		Et	as usual. —
10	4			EbS	Gannets. Tropic Gulls. and Flying Fish. —
11	4				
12	3	4		EdS.	Moderate with showers and fair Intervals — Served 1/24 lb.
	106				Bread. and Water for Dinner. —
	3693				
	3/99		Meridn Altd		
			☉ Center } Sd.. 23		

				Latitude	Longitude
Course	Dist	Obs.	DR	DR	
WNW¾W	106	S.. 45 S	S.. 45 S	135.. 16 Et	

Journal.

This day the Sea run very high and we were very wet: suffering much Cold in the Night — I now remarked that the Surgeon Mr. Ledward and an Old hardy Seaman Lawrence Lebogue. giving way very fast. — I could only afsist them by a teaspoonfull or two of Wine at day light. — Amongst most of the others I observe more than a common inclination to Sleep a Symptom of Nature being almost reduced to its last effort. —

Served 1/24 lb. Bread. and a Gill of Water at Supper Breakfast and Dinner — Saw several Gannets and Signs of land which lies to the Northward of us. —

H	K	F	Course	Winds	Rem.ᵈ Tuesday 9ᵗʰ June 1789. Bounty's Launch. Towards Timor
1	3	4	NWbS	ENE.	Moderate with some Showers and fair Intervals. —
2	4	2		to	
3	4			SE.	
4	3		~	~	Caught a Small Dolphin - Ifsued about 2 oz to each Man including
5	4	2			the Offals and directed the remainder to be kept for tomorrow's dinner. —
6	4	2	~	SEbS	
7	4				
8	4				
9	4	4			
10	4	2			
11	4	2			
12	4	2	~	~	Fresh Gale Shipping much Water and constantly bailing. —
1	5				
2	5				
3	5				
4	5				
5	5				
6	5		~	SE	Very Wet and Cold Served the Surgeon and Lebogue a little Wine. —
7	5				Miserable complaints
8	5		~	~	Served Bread and Water for Breakfast as before
9	4	4			Gannets - Boobies - Men of War Birds and Tropic Gulls. —
10	5				
11	4	4	~	SEbE	
12	5		~	~	Fine Wʳ and a fresh Gale — Shipping much Water and bailing, but
	109				it is a blefsing that we are going on so rapidly. —
3	109				Served 72⁴ ℔. Bread, and Water with the remainder of the Dolphin
3	3.27		Meridⁿ Altᵈ ⊙ Center } 57..53		which amounted to an Oz pʳ Man.

			Latitude		Longitude
Course	Disᵗ	Obsᵈ		DR	DR
S 76 W	107	9..09 S		S.. 56 S	133..31 E

Journal

Towards Evening of this day the Wind began to freshen again and continued to blow Strong from the SE, so that we continued to ship much Water and suffer wet and Cold. —

At 4 this afternoon we caught a small Dolphin which is the first relief of the kind we have had. Issued about 2 oz to each person including the Offals, and saved the remainder for Dinner. —

At Day Light I as usual heard and felt very miserable complaint. — I gave the Surgeon and Lebogue a little Wine, but I could give no farther relief than assurances that a few Days would bring us to Timor, and that were to consider at the fine Rate we were going on and endeavor to bear with our situation. —

Gannets — Boobies — Men of War Birds and Tropic Gulls constantly about us. —

Served the usual allowance of Bread and Water and at Noon we dined on the remainder of the Dolphin which amounted to about 1 oz pr. Man. —

H	K	F	Courses	Winds	Remᵏˢ Wednesday 10ᵗʰ June 1789 Bounty's Launch towᵈˢ Timor
1	5		W.½S	S.b.E.	Fresh Gales and fine Wr. — Much Sea.
2	5				
3	5				
4	4	2			(Birds as Yesterday) —
5	4	2			
6	4	4	..	..	Served ¹⁄24 lb Bread and a Gill of Water for Supper —
7	4	4			Constantly Wet and bailing. —
8	4	4			
9	4	6			
10	4				
11	4				
12	4		..	..	Very Wet and Cold.
1	4		..	E.S.E.	
2	4				
3	4				
4	4				
5	4	4			
6	4	4	..	..	Very Wet and Cold — Miserable Complaints
7	5				
8	4	4	..	..	Served ¹⁄24 lb Bread and a Gill of Water for Breakfast
9	4	6			Birds as Yesterday.
10	4	4			
11	4	4			
12	4	4	..	..	Strong Trade and much Sea — Constantly bailing. Served ¹⁄24 lb Bread & Water for Dinner. —

111
33 00
31 19   Merid Altᵈ / O Center } 57..41

Course		Latitude		Longitude
	Dist	Obsᵈ	DR	DR
W.½S	111	9..16 S	9..16 S	131..30 E

Journal

Fresh Gales and fair W.r but a continuance of much Sea. which by breaking almost constantly over us, we are miserably Wet and suffer much Cold in the Night

This Afternoon I suffered a prodigious Sickness from the Oily Nature of part of the Stomach of the Fish which had fallen to my lot at Dinner. —// At Sun Down I served an Allowance of Bread and Water for Supper, and in the Morning after a miserable Night I began to see an Alteration for the Worse with more than half my people. whose looks rather indicated an approaching end to their distresses. — They Received of Bread and Water for Breakfast and Dinner. —

H	K	F	Courses	Winds	Rem.s Thursday 11.th June 1789. Bountys Launch Towards Timor
1	4		W½S	. E	Strong Trade and fair Wr. much Sea constantly bailing. —
2	4				
3	3	6	"	"	Many Gannets and Boobies. —
4	4				
5	4	6			
6	4	4	"	"	Served ¼ lb Bread. and a Gill of Water for Supper.
7	4	2			
8	4	2	WbS		
9	4	4			
10	4	6			
11	4	4			
12	5				
1	5				
2	5				
3	4	4			
4	4	4		SbE	Miserably Wet and Cold.
5	4	4			
6	4	4			
7	4	4	"	"	Saw pieces of Rock Weed and Gannets
8	4	4	"	"	Served ¼ lb Bread. and a Gill of Water for Breakfast. and Wrung
9	4				and dryed our Wet Cloaths. — Served the Surgeon and Lawe Lebogue
10	3	6			a little Wine
11	4				
12	3	6	"	"	Moderate and fine Wr. but remarkably hazy. Served ¼ lb Bread and
	107				a Gill of Water or two for dinner. —
3	4	9			People begin to appear very much on the decline Lawe Lebogue and
35	26				the Surgeon cannot live a Week longer if I do not get relief. —

Course	Dist.	Latitude		Longitude
		Obs.d	DR	DR
S77W	109	9°..41 S	9°..24 S	129°..50 E

Journal

Birds and Rock Weed shew us we are not far from Land, but I know such signs must be here, as a long string of Islands stretch to the Eastward from Timor towards New Guinea, I however hope to fall in with Timor every hour, or else I have scarce a hope but I shall lose some of my People. — An extreme Weakness. — Swelled Legs — hollow and Ghastly countenances. — great propensity to sleep and an apparent debility of Understanding; give me melancholy proofs of an approaching dissolution. — The Surgeon and an Old hardy Seaman Law.ce Lebogue are indeed miserable Objects, I issue to them a few tea spoonfulls of Wine out of the little I have preserved for this dreadfull Stage, and it seems to help and may secure their existence a little longer. For my own part a great share of spirits and no doubt of being to accomplish the Voyage seems to be my principal Support; but the Boatswain when I was rallying him to day, very innocently told me that he realy thought I looked Worse than any one in the Boat. the simplicity however with which he uttered such an Opinion diverted me, and I had good humour enough to return him a better Compliment

Every one received his 1/24 lb. of Bread and a Gill of Water. At Evening Morning and Noon and those who wish for an extra allowance of Water get it

At Noon allowing the East End of Timor to be 128d..00 East my distance from it is only 33 leagues. this diffused a Universal joy and satisfaction. —

H	K	F	Courses	Winds	Rem.ˢ Friday 12ᵗʰ June 1789. Bountys Launch. Towards Timor
1	4	..	W½S	SEbS	Fine Wʳ but exceedingly hazy.
2	4				
3	4		„	SE	
4	4		„	„	Gannets and many Tropic Gulls.– Caught a Booby by hand. which
5	4		West		ordered to be kept for Dinner. —
6	4		„	„	Issued 724 lb Bread, and two Gills of Water. to each person.. I hourly
7	4	4		East	expect to fall in with Timor and have a most anxious look out
8	4	6			
9	5				
10	5				
11	4	4			
12	5				
1	5				
2	5				
3	4	6	„	„	With an excep of Joy we discovered Timor bearing WNW. to WbS.
4	3		NNE.		Hauled the Wind.
5	3				At Day light. Timor from SWbS. 2 leagˢ low land to NE½N
6	3		SbE.	EbS.	7 leagˢ interior part Mountainous. —
7	3		SbW.	„	At ½ Coast opening to the Southᵈ with the low land at SW.– Bore away
8	3		SSW.	„	Very Hazy Wʳ the extremes of Timor from SWbW. 5 leagˢ to NEbN
9	3				6 leagˢ– and the low land set at day light NbW. 3 Miles. —
10	3		„	„	High head lands opend. with the south. as set at Dᵃ SW½W.
11	3		SWbS.	SE.	
12	3		„	„	Fresh Breezes and hazy..– The low land seen at day light is now
95					the East extreme bearing NNE½E. 4 leagˢ: The South extreme set at
35	26				Dᵃ NbE½E. 3 Miles and the South.ᵗ land in sight SW½W. 5 leagˢ:
36	21		Meridⁿ Altᵈ }	° ′	Land Mountainous and Woody. —
			⊙ Center }	56..50	

			Latitude		Longitude	
Course	Distᵗ	Obsᵈ	DR	DR		
S76.W	77..	9..59 S	9..51 S	120..33 Eᵗ		

Journal

All the Afternoon we had several Gannets and many Birds about that indicated we were near to Land, and at Sun Down we had a very anxious look out.—

At 3 in the Morning with an excess of Joy we discovered Timor bearing WSW to WNW and I hauled the Wind to the NNE. untill day light when the land bore from SWBS about 2 Leag.s to NEBN. 7 leagues ——

At 7.h I bore away along the South East side of the Island steering SSW and SWBS.— At Noon the extremes of Timor from SW½W. 5 Leagues to NNE½E. 4 leagues.— Distant off shore 3 Miles.— The Sun being to the Northward of me. I fear my Latitude may not be very exact being so near the Land.—

It is not possible for me to describe the joy that the blessing of seeing the Land diffused among us—indeed it is scarce within the scope of belief that in 41 days I could be on the Coast of Timor in which time we have run by our Log 3623 Miles which on a Medium is 90 Miles a Day.—

I have already mentioned I knew not at what part of the Island the Dutch Settlement was and I was still at a loss, but I had a presentiment that it was at the SW part. I therefore steered to the Southward along the South shore of the Island with more satisfaction, for I could not go on the North without some loss of time.—

The Day gave us an agreeable prospect of the Land. which was interspersed with Woods and Lawns. the interior part Mountainous, but the Shore low. Towards Noon the Coast became higher, and we were highly delighted with the general look of the Country which exhibited cultivated Spots and many beautifull; but we could only see a few Small Hutts, from whence I concluded no European resided at this part of the Island.—Much Sea run on the Shore. so that the landing with a Boat was im= =practicable—I found I was on the SE side as the point of the Coast came in sight in the direction of SW.—

In the Evening we caught a Booby which I reserved for our Dinners, but I had some difficulty to stop the Masters muttering because I would not serve it for Breakfast, for this ignorant Man conceived he was instantly to be in the midst of Plenty—The Allowance of Bread and Water I issued as before, & to the Surgeon and Leboque I gave a little Wine.——

H	K	F	Courses	Winds	Rem.ᵈ Saturday 13ᵗʰ June 1789. Bountys Launch. Timor
1	3	6	SW	NEbE	Fair W. and hazy with Moderate Breezes.
2	3	6	WSW		
3	3	4	SW		
4	4		WSW	EbE.	The south.ᵈ point of land in sight WBS 4 Miles but could see high land
5	5		WBS		over it at a distance in the same direction – A High Cape land bore
6	5				NE 3/4 E and is the SE Cape of this Island – My distance Off Shore 2 Miles
7	"		} Up SSE		At Sun set the extremes from WBS 1/2 S 6 leagues to East 5 Miles Off
8	.				Shore 1 1/2 Mile – Served 1/24 lb Bread, and Water for Supper. –
9	.			East	At 6 Hove too under the Foresail for the Night lest I might pass any
10	.		Off SSW		settlement. –
11	.				
12	..				
1	"		} Do		
2	.			..	At 2 Wore and hove too head in shore
3	.		}		
4	.		Up NEbN		
5	..		Off N bW	EbE	Strong Gale and Squally. Served Bread & Water for breakfast
6	9		WBS.		At 6 I found I had drifted about WbS 3 leagues. Made Sail. –
7	4	6	W1/2 S	EbS	Land opening at West with the West extreme set last Night. –
8	4	6	..	..	The West Extreme set at S last night NW 2 Miles, and Western.ᵈ land
9	4	4	West.	EbE	in Sight W1/2 S – A Weather Current and much Sea. –
10	4	4	..	..	Saw Mountainous Land SW 6 or 7 leag.ˢ to SWbW1/2 W I believe an Isl.ᵈ
11	2	4	W1/2 N	SE	
12	2	4	..	..	Fresh Gales and very hazy. W. – The Island as before and the Westermost part of the Main in Sight WBSbS 3 leag.ˢ No Observ – a half mile from the Shore. Served Bread & Water for Dinner as Usual. –

50
36 2 1
36 7 9

Course	Dist	Obs.ᵈ	Latitude DR	Longitude DR	Rem.ᵈ
S77W	54	None	10..12 S	127..38 E	Latitude this Noon reduced back 10..20 S

At Sun set after running to the W.S.W. 25 Miles I hove too for the Night— The extremes of the Land, from W.b.S ½ S. 6 Leag.s to East. 5 Miles, off shore about ½ Mile— we were here in Shoal Water.— Served Bread and Water for Supper. and the Boat lying too very Well under the Reefed Lug Foresail. All but the Officer of the Watch endeavored to get a little Sleep.—

At 2 in the Morning I wore and Stood in shore untill day light, When I found. we had not drifted more than 3 leagues to the W.b.S, the Southermost land bearing West, in the direction of which I made Sail along Shore, with a Weather Current and much Sea.—

At Noon. High Mountainous Land bore S.W.b.W. 7 leagues off. and the South part of Timor W.b.S ½ S about 3 leagues.—I had no Observation for the latitude.— The usual allowance of Bread and Water I issued for Breakfast and Dinner, and to the Surgeon and Leboque I gave a little Wine.—

During the Afternoon I continued my Course along a low Woody Shore with innumerable Palm Trees called the Fan Palm owing to the leaf spreading like a Fan, But we had lost all signs of Cultivation, and the Country had not so fine an Appearance as it had before. towards the S.E. Cape which is a high head land,— This however was only a small tract of Country, for by Sun down it improved again and I saw several large Smokes where the Malays were clearing and cultivating their grounds.—

At Sun set I was West five Miles from a low point which I had considered as southermost land in the afternoon, and here the Coast formed a deep bend with low land in the Bight I conceived to be Islands. The West Shore was high but from hence to the S.E Cape the shore is low, and I believe Shoal from the S.E Cape to the Westward.—

I remark particularly this situation, because here the very high Ridge of Mountains that run from the East end of the Island. terminates; and the Eye is abruptly effected with a Sudden change of Country, as if it was not the same Island. in any one respect.—It nevertheless continues to be high land, but apparently much inferior in Value.—

That I might not commit a blunder in the Night by running past any settlement—I determined to preserve my Station untill the Morning, and I therefore hove too under a Close Refed Foresail, with which the Boat performed Wonderfully Well.

At Day light on examining the Coast I found I had farther to go in search of a settlement, and I bore away with a Strong Gale along a high Shore covered with Wood. but no signs of Cultivation.—

Low land now again began to appear with the points of the Coast opening at West I was therefore certain of being on the South part of the Island, when at 10 OClock I saw high land from SW. to SW.b W.½ W and the Coast I was on as far as NSW.½ W, but the Weather was so prodigiously hazy that it became doubtfull to me. whether the two lands were seperated, the Opening only extending one point of the Compass I for this reason stood towards the outer land and found it to be the Island Rotty, when I returned to the Shore I had left and in a sandy Bay. I brought to a Grapnel — In this place we saw several Smokes of Clearing Land, and the Master and Carpenter having been troublesome and asserted I kept them from getting Supplies, I gave them leave to quit the Boat but the others who had ever been too obedient to disobey my Orders. I directed to remain, so that finding no One to be of their party they chose to be excused. I lost not a Moments time here, than to calculate my situation and Steering alongshore I had a view of a pretty looking Country as if formed by Art into Lawns and Parks. — The shore is all low land covered with Wood, among which are innumerable Fan Palm Trees that look like Cocoa Nutt Walks. The interior part is high land but very different from the more Eastern parts of the Island. where it is exceedingly Mountainous and better soil. —

H	K	F	Courses	Winds	Rems. Sunday 14th June 1789 Bountys Launch Timor
1	4		West	ESE	Strong Gales and very hazey Wr. and a high dangerous breaking Sea
2	4				
3	1		North		Came to a Grapnel (on the West end of Timor) in the Entrance of
4			NEbN		a large Inlet in a Bay on the East side from whence the Islands
5					without bore SBW ¾ W. to SW ¾ W. 5 leags. the West point of the Entrance
6					W½ S 3 Miles and the SE point SBW. ¾ Mile — Modt & fair Wr
7			NE	SE	Saw a Dog and some Cattle — Sent the Boatswain & Gunner in
8			NEbE	East	search of Inhabitants. — At 4 they returned with some Malay
9				Calm	Men, one of whom agreed to shew me where the Governor resided
10	8			NE	who he called Bassar and the place Coupang. —
11				Calm	At ½ past 4 left this place, and kept the East side of the Bay
12					on board. sailing and Rowing with light Airs. —
1				SE	At 10 Came to a Grapnel. Light airs
2			NEbE		At 1 o'Clock Weighed and pulled along the East and South
3					shore and found the land I had been passing on the West to be
4			ENE		an Island, we being now open to the Sea. No Ground at 10 fm.
5	5		East		At Day dawn came to a Grapnel under the Fort at Coupang
6					and hoisted a Small Jack we had made in the Main Shrouds
7					as a Signal of distress. —
8					At 6 I had leave to land.
9					At 9 I got every one on shore
10					
11					
12					Modt and Fair Wr found lying in the Road. One large Ship
	22				a Snow and a Dutch Cutter. —
	3	79			Got the Boat hauled into the River. —
	37	01			

Mean Course from 4 to 10 PM NEbE — 8
Do   Do — from 1 to 5 AM ENE 5

Course	Dist	Latitude		Longitude
		Obs	DK	DK
N 27 E	9	10 .. 12	10 .. 04 S	127 .. 42 E

At 2 O'Clock this Afternoon after having run through a very dangerous Sea the Cause of which I attributed to a Strong Windward Tide and Shoal Water We discovered a Spacious Bay or Sound with a fair Entrance about 2 or 3 miles Wide. — I now conceived Hopes that my Voyage was nearly at an End, as no place could Appear more elligible for Shipping. and of Course likely to be the Dutch Settlement. I therefore bore up and Came to a Grapnel on the East Side of the Entrance in a small Sandy Bay where we Saw a Hut a Dog and some Cattle, and I immediatly Sent the Boatswain and Gunner away to the Hut in Order to discover the Inhabitants

The SW point of the Entrance bore W½S 3 Miles. the SE part SbW½ Mile and the Island. Rotty from SbW¼ W to SW¼ W about 5 leagues off. —

While I lay here I found the Tide of Ebb to come from the Northward, and before I came away showed a dangerous Rocky Reef about 2 Cables length from the Shore that took the direction of this Side of the Entrance and the whole being covered at high Water renders it dangerous. On the other side also appeared very high Breakers, but here is nevertheless plenty of Room and most certainly a Safe Channel for a first Rate.

The Bay or Sound within is of a Considerable extent, the Northern part which I had now in view being about 5 leags distant. Here the Land made on moderate risings, joined by lower Grounds. — But the Island which lies to the South is the best mark to know this place by, and Is what I consider to be the Island Rotty or Rotto. —

I had just time to make these remarks when I saw the Boatswain and Gunner returning with some Malays, I therefore no longer doubted of my Success, and our most sanguine expectations and Wishes were fully gratified They brought five Malay Men with them, and informed me they had found two families where the Women treated them with European politeness, and that the Men had by Signs given them to understand, that the Governor resided at some distance to the NE. — Their intercourse with the Dutch did not remain one moment a doubt to me, but I could only make out Bassar and Coupang, the former I understood to be the Governors Name and the latter his residence. — I now made Signs for One of them to go in the

Boat and shew me Coupang, intimating that I would pay money for his trouble, when the Man readily complied and came into the Boat. —

These People were of a dark tawny Colour, and had long black Hair, Chewed a great deal of Beetle, and wore a Square piece of foreign Cloth round their Hips in the folds of which was stuck a large Knife. They had a Handkerchief wrapt round their heads, and at their shoulders hung another tied by the four Corners, which constituted a Bag for their Beetle Equipage. —

The only thing they brought us was a few dried pieces of Turtle that was not eatable untill Soaked in Hot water, and a few Ears of Indian Corn. — This last was a treasure to us, and had I stayed they would have brought us something more; but as the Pilot was willing I determined to push on, and I sailed about half past four. —

By the direction of the Pilot I kept the East shore on board under all our Sail, but as Night came on the Wind died away, and we were obliged to try at the Oars which I was surprized to find we could do with some effect. — However at 10 Oclock as I found we got but little ahead I came to a Grapnel, and for the first time I issued about double Allowance of Bread and a little Wine to each person. — At One Oclock in the Morning after the most happy & sweetest Sleep that ever Men had, I weighed and continued to keep the East shore on board in very Smooth Water, when at last I found we were again Open to the Sea, the whole of the Land to the Westward that I had passed being a large Island which the Pilot called Pulo Samow. — In this North Entrance it is about 1½ or 2 Miles wide, and I had no ground at 10 fms —

Hearing the report of two Cannon that were fired gave new life to every One and before day we discovered two Square Rigged Vessels and a Cutter at Anchor to the Eastward. — I endeavored to Work to Windward but we were obliged to take to our Oars again having lost ground on every tack, and having kept Close to the Shore we continued rowing untill 4 O'Clock when I brought to a Grapnel and gave another allowance of Bread and Wine to all hands, and being refreshed we again rowed untill an half hour before Day, when I came to a Grapnel off a Small Fort & Town called Coupang. —

When the Boatswain left the Ship, among the things he had thrown into the Boat was a bundle of Signal Flags that I had made for the Boats to shew me the depth of Water in Sounding. — These I had in the Course of this Miserable Voyage converted into a Small Jack which I now hoisted in the Main Shrouds as a Signal of distress, for I did not for very evident reasons chuse to land without leave. — Soon after day break a soldier hailed me to land, which I instantly did among a Crowd of Malays, and I was agreeably surprized to meet with an English sailor who belonged to the ship in the Road. — His Captain he told me was the second Person in the Town I therefore desired to be Conducted to him as I found the Governor was Ill and could not just then be Spoke with

Captain Spykerman received me with great humanity, and being informed of my miserable situation, I requested that I might have assistance and that care might be taken of those who were with me without delay. — He therefore gave directions for their immediate victualling in his Own House, and went himself to the Governor to know at what time I could be permitted to see him, which was fixed to be at Eleven O'Clock. —

I now desired every one to come on shore, which was as much as some of them could do being scarce able to Walk they however got at last to the House and had Tea with Bread and Butter for their Breakfasts. —

The abilities of the most eminent Artists perhaps could never have more brilliantly shone than in a delineation of two Groups of Figures that at this time presented themselves, and when one might be so much at a loss to know which most to admire, whether the Eyes of Famine sparkling at immediate relief, or their Preserver horror struck at the Spectres of Men. — For any one to Conceive the picture of such poor Miserable Beings, let him fancy that in his House he is in the moment of giving relief to Eighteen Men whose ghastly countenances, but from the known Cause would be equally liable to affright as demand pity; let him view their Limbs full of Sores and their Bodies nothing but Skin and Bones habited in Rags, and at last let him Conceive he sees the Tears of Joy and gratitude flowing O'er their Cheeks at their Benefactors. — With the mixture of horror surprize and pity that his Mind will be then agitated, were the People of Timor on giving us releif. —

The Governor Mr. Willem Adriaan Van Este notwithstanding extreme ill health became so anxious to give us releif, that I saw him before the appointed time. — He received me with great affection, and gave me the most demon=strative proofs of being possessed of every feeling of a humane and good Man. — Sorry as he was he said, that such a calamity could ever have happened to me, Yet he considered it as the Greatest blessing of his life that I had fallen under his protection, and altho his infirmity was so great that he could not do the Office of a Friend him=self, Yet he would issue such Orders as I might be certain would cause me to effect every Supply I wanted, in the Mean time a House was hired for me, and untill Matters could be properly regulated Victuals for every one were to be dressed at his own House. With respect to my people he said I might have room for them either at the Hospital or on board of Captain Spykermans Ship which lay in the Road, and expressed much uneasyness that Coupang could not give them better acco=modations, the House I was to have being the only one uninhabited, and the situation of the few families were such that they could not accomodate any one These things I had therefore to consider of, I was however more disposed to talk of business than this Gentleman, whose feelings tortured him with my extreme Wants and distress, to the releif of which, an elegant repast was put before me as the Custom of the Country more than through design to alleviate my hunger, so that in this instance he happily blended in common politeness the greatest favor I could receive. —

On my return to my people I found every kind releif had been given to them. The Surgeon had dressed their Sores, and the Cleaning of their Persons were not less attended to, with several friendly Gifts of Apparel

I now desired to be shewn the House that was intended for me, & I found it ready with Servants to attend and a particular one which the Governor had directed to be always about my person. — The House consisted of a Hall with a Room at each end and a loft over head, and all round a Piazza, with an outer Apartment in one Corner, and a communication from the back part of the House to the Street. I therefore determined instead of letting my People out of my Sight, to take them all with me, and I instantly divided the House as follows – One Room I took to my self & the other I allotted to the Master, Doctor Mʳ Nelson the Botanist, and the Gunner. – the Loft to the other Officers; and the outer Apartment to the Men. The Hall was common to all the Officers, and the Men had the back Piazza. – Of this I informed the Governor and he sent down Chairs, Tables, Benches and other Necessaries for the use of every one with some Articles of Bedding –

I had promised the Governor on my leaving him, as it was his particular request, that he should be acquainted with every thing I stood in Want of; but I now found it was only at particular times that he had a few Moments of ease, and could attend to any thing, being in a dying State with an incurable fistula. – For this reason all my transactions of business I found would be with a Mʳ Timotheus Wanjon the second of this place. the Governors Son in Law, who now also was contributing every way in his power to make our situation happy and agreeable. – I was therefore misinformed by the Seaman that Captʳ Spykerman was the next principal person to the Governor

At Noon a very handsome Dinner was brought to the House which was sufficient to make persons more accustomed to plenty to eat too much, cautions therefore on that Head may be supposed to have had little effect, but I believe few people in such a situation could have observed more moderation The greatest danger I was apprehensive of was their getting Fruit –

Having seen every one enjoy this Meal of plenty I dined with Mʳ Wanjon, but I found no extraordinary inclination to eat or drink, or did I find my Stomach able to bear any thing altho every article was most kindly thought of that was fit for me to make use of – Rest and quietness I considers the most necessary ingredients to my doing Well, and I therefore retired to my Room which I found furnished with every convenience. — But instead of rest, I found my mind more disposed to reflect on the sufferings I had gone through, of the failure of my expedition, but above all of the thanks due to Almighty God who had given me power to support and bear such heavy Calamities, and to enable me at last to be the means of Saving 18 Lives which would never otherwise have been thought of —

My situation as a Commander became burthened with more than mere bodily distresses for besides what will readily be believed (with respect to me) such as directing and pointing out the Route we were to go; I had to oblige every one to drag on a lingering life with a miserable allowance of support, and to find repeatedly the melancholy request of "Give us more Bread" combating a necessary resolution of refusal. — This I so sacredly stuck to that I brought eleven days allowance in with me, it is therefore evident that the least degree of inattention or want of care in the distribution of this Article would have put an end to our existence; but from a strict adherence to the agreement we set out with; it is equally certain if I had missed Timor, I could have pursued my Voyage to Java where at Passourwang or Sourabaya (from information I had got at the Cape of Good Hope. I knew I could get every thing I wanted. —

Among the many melancholy circumstances that attend a Commander in my late Situation, is the Caprice and Ideas of ignorant people. Voraciousness had I been incapable of acting would have carried the Boat on shore as soon as I had made the Island, without considering or knowing that Landing among the Malays might be as bad as among any other Indians But exclusive of the Fatigue of the Mind, to reflect on what I have in common undergone, I appear to be contemplating a Dream rather than a reality with the facts staring me in the Face —

When I reflect how providentialy our lives were saved at Tofoa by the Indians delaying their attack, and that with scarce any thing for forty Eight Days to support life we have crossed a Sea of more than 1200 leagues without shelter from the inclemency or protection from the Evils of the Climates   When I reflect how natural it was to be expected that disease might have taken most of us off, besides the great probability of foundering at Sea, and when I view the great good fortune we had to pass the unfriendly Natives of other Countries without accident, and at last happily to meet with the most friendly and best of People to relieve our distresses, it calls up a distracted mind of astonishment, and most humble gratitude and reverence to Almighty God. — Through such blessings only could I bear with the failure of an expedition on which I had so much set my mind had completed so far with such extraordinary Success; and to which my King and the Honorable Promoters of so great and extensive a Charity, I consider are regarding with great satisfaction and pleasure. —

    With respect to our own endeavors to preserve health during a Course of 16 Days heavy and almost continual Rain, I could only recommend to every one to pull of their Cloaths and wring them out of the Sea Water as often as they became filled with Rain, and it was the only resource We had for dry cloaths, but we at last wrung all our Cloaths to pieces for except the few days on the Coast of New Holland there never was any person who was not wet with Rain or Sea. —

    Thus happily ended through the assistance of Divine Providence without accident a Voyage of the most extraordinary Nature that ever happened in the World., let it be taken in its extent duration and so much want of the Necessaries of Life.

The following Diary will be kept according to Civil Account beginning the Day at Midnight

---

Remarks at Coupang in Timor Monday 15th June 1789. —

Fair W.r with light land Winds at Night and strong Sea Breezes from ESE and SE. from 9 in the Morning to 3 in the Afternoon. —

Altho the Night was passed happily different from any we had at Sea, Yet we found ourselves very little refreshed, a circumstance which often happens to People when extremely fatigued; but to this perhaps we may attribute the Sleeping without Beds as an additional cause. — The few People that are here have only Birds for themselves, I therefore only got a Neat Bedstead with two Quilts for a Mattrass and a Counterpain from the Governor, whose goodness I am sure would have done more for my Sore bones, if Beds were to be had. — The Officers and Men were mostly obliged to make Guard Beds with what came with us which however I might not expect, was thought of no Moment among the People here. —

As I went through some fatigue Yesterday in arranging matters for the Comfort and reception of those who were with me, it was now produc-ing some ill effects which it was necessary to guard against, a Slight Fever however with Severe head ach were the most alarming Symptoms. — Every one complained of a want of evacuation by Stool. — Tenesmus became extreme and the excruciating torture from not being able to void the faecis perhaps was more than ever experienced in the World. — Vast Weakness succeeded this with Gripings and Cholick Complaints, besides swelled legs and irritated Sores that we got at Tofoa, so that not a person but what was under the

Doctor's Care — This Gentleman recommended as the best Physician to eat Moderately and abstain from fruit untill the Stomach had acquired its usual tone, but some already had begun to completely satisfy their Appetite which produced very severe Cholick Complaints or rather uncommon pains in the Bowels. —

At Noon a very plentifull and good Dinner

was sent to the House; and as I was confined by a severe indisposition every thing was thought of that could be of service to me.—

I find the Europeans of this Place are.

Willem Adriaan Van Este.—: Koopman. & Opperhooft. Governor.

Timotheus. Wanjon . . . . . Secunde.

Frug — . — — — Secretary.

Max — . — — — . Surgeon.

Temminck — — . — Minister

Gans — — — — — Ensign. and 30 Soldiers . —

Van Es — . — : — — — Merchant.

A Surgeons Mate.

A few others of little Note —

The rest. of the Inhabitants are Malays and Chinese. —

Remarks in Coupang Tuesday 16th June 1789. —

Fine Wr with light Winds at Night and strong Winds S Ely in the day.

Gripings and Vomiting were the Complaints among us at this time. — Myself became attacked with a Fever and could keep nothing on my Stomach, every thing was thought of by Mr Van Este and Mr Wanjon that could be of any Service, and the Doctor Mr Max and his Second attended us with vast Kindness and attention. — I found great relief from keeping my Legs in Warm Water about an half hour every Evening Those who were able were Ordered to bath every Morning before Sun Rise in a fine Fresh Water River, and to every one gentle exercise was recom- mended in the cool of the day, and I therefore Ordered every one to attend at the Doctors at his time of business at the Hospital. —

Remarks in Coupang 17th and 18th June 1789. —

  Fine Wr. with Land and Sea Breezes as on the 16th —

  Every one continues very weak and subject to the same complaints as before which are in a great Measure to eating to much — I am still confined with a Fever. — I received a Message to day from Mr. Van Este informing me he was suffering such extreme torture and was reduced so low that it was out of his Power to see me. — Mr. Wanjon was however ready to render me any Service. —

Remarks in Coupang. Friday 19th June 1789.

Fair W.r with Land and Sea Breezes. with Calms. —

Every person is now beginning to recover except myself. — Great Weak- ness and Fever still hangs about me. which keeps me confined. A little Sago is the only thing my Stomach can bear. —

Cold Meat or Fish with Rice for Breakfast. — Broth and Boulie and other Meat. stewed or variously dressed for Dinner and nearly the same for Supper is the common way that every one is fed. —

I ordered every one to be supplied to day with Slops, such as could be got at this place but all are at a great price at least one hundred pr Cent dearer than at Batavia. — Their situation however made it necessary to take them at any price. —

Wind and Weather as Yesterday and a Charming fine Air. —

Myself and some others still continue very Weak, but upon the whole the generality of us are gathering Strength very fast —

I receive the kindest enquiries from Mr Van Este how we are going on, and the most constant personal attention from Mr Wanjon. — a genteel Table is always kept for me, and every person is fed in a plentifull Manner. —

On Sunday Morning for the first time I found myself able to go out, I therefore directed every one to go to Church where I attended to return thanks to Almighty God for his late gracious protection and preservation of our lives. — The Chapel is exceedingly neat and the Congregation consisted of about 50 persons most of whom were Malays. —

In General the Malay language is spoken here and the Church Service in the Afternoon is always read by a Malay.

The peculiar civility of Mr Wanjon obliged me to dine with him to day, and through him as Mr Van Este's extreme ill health renders him incapable, I am to transact all business. — .

Remarks in Company Monday 22nd June 1789. —

Moderate and fine pleasant Wr. Wind ESE. Calm in the Night. —

I began to day to feel my health returning to me and my living is changed to a use of more solids — some of my Company are become unwell from having eaten too much. — The sore Feet and Legs of some are troublesome to heal, they are however getting tolerably on and begin to lose their ghastly meagre Countenances. —

The Governor having given me the use of a Horse induced me to take a Small Ride into the Country which I found to be very Rocky, a shallow burnt up Soil; and but few places worth or fit for any kind of Cultivation. — The Roads or more properly beaten paths are very bad, being very rocky and encumbered with Bushes

One Mile and a half along the Sea side to the Northward of the Town is a pretty Spot of Garden Ground called Owar the property of Mr Wanjon who uses it as his Country residence — The Cocoa Nutt Trees grow very luxuriantly and the fruit large, of which they make but little use than for Oil. — Other fine fruits & peculiarities of this Country are here; but as a Kitchen Garden there was but little in it worth notice. — The Trees which produce the Beetle Nutt, called Penang, grow luxuriantly here, they appear to me to be exactly like what we Call the Mountain Cabbage Tree in the West Indies, which Mr Nelson could not ascertain, as with the latter he told me he was not acquainted. — The Fruit which is the Size of a Nutmeg and not unlike it, is coated like the Cocoa Nutt, and they grow in bunches from the Tree where the soft green part of the Top begins. — Several very extraordinary and curious Trees were here also of that Genus that encrease their Trunks by Shooting out long strings which on reaching the Ground take Root, and by degrees connect with one another and make a compact body of an incredible size. With a Small degree of Art one of these Trees might be made to spread an Acre of Ground with most Romantick and Curious Arch Ways. — I saw two Bread fruit Trees but no Fruit on them. — This Pretty Spot is finely watered by a Natural Fountain and has a small Fish Pond with many Carp in it.

The Sea shore is formed by Sandy Bays and low Rocky heads, and at low Water in some places give a half Mile of flat Rocky ground where Dams are made to catch Fish. — I saw in my Road to Owar several Malay Graves. These People I find perform some peculiar Rites to the deceased as on some of the Graves I saw small baskets with Tobacco & Beetle —

Fair Wr. with light E S E Winds

It was a Matter at first of great concern to me that neither Mr. Van Este or Mr. Wanjon spoke English or French, but fortunately there happened to be a Gentleman of the Faculty (Mr. Hendrick Arnold. Daniel Mertz) who had come from Batavia to endeavor to render some Service to Mr. Van Este, who spoke English very well to him I applyed on all Occasions, when I had any business to transact and he readily rendered us every Service that way. —

I find this is the only settlement of the Dutch on this Island. — It was formerly, I am told a place of Plenty and a tolerable Trade, but that at present every thing is scarce and very dear, their Trade was Bees Wax and Sandle Wood. — At this time only one Ship is sent here by the Company, and is with some difficulty loaded. — The Island. they affect is almost robbed of all its Sandle Wood, Yet a Large Brig and a Sloop find it worth their while to Trade here under Private Merchants, altho the Company cannot make much of it. —

The Scarcity of every thing here induced me to come to an agreement to Pay for every except myself for Board & Lodgings at the rate of 36 Stivers pr. Day and for myself 2½ Rex Dollars pr. Day as I found this would be more advantageous than any other Way of proceeding. —

Fine pleasant W.^r with light Easterly Winds with Calms in the Night or land Breezes.

Several beside myself continue in a very Weak State but as we are supplied with every nourishing Article that is necessary there is little doubt of our doing Well.

This is not the time of Year for abundance of Fruit there are however some in season — I had sent me some very fine Anonas or the Custard Apple of Jamaica and a few Pomegranates. the Otaheiteans have a fruit they call Nona, but it is as unpleasant as the Custard Apple is agreeable. —

The Governor notwithstanding his ill health and extreme pain which he suffers in general, had a trifling intermission this Evening by which means I had the pleasure of seeing him by invitation, so peculiarly anxious is he to know if I have every thing as it should be, altho at the same time he is sensible of Mr Wanjon great attention to all my Wants. —

In speaking of the scarcity of Provisions I was told the Cause of it in part was occasioned by a War among the Natives which took place in 1786 & lasted untill 1788. — The Chief of this Island has the Title of Keyser or Emperor given him by the Dutch and his Malay Subjects being numerous he is of course of consequence among the Europeans. — ~~But the reason they~~ There are some others who from the Power they possess are dangerous Subjects so that the seeds of discord being sown they formed a design of Revolution and openly brought forward a Usurper who was Nephew to the present Emperor. —

As I have mentioned before this is the only Settlement the Dutch have at this Island if we except a few People who are dispersed about the Country as residents to regulate any little business that may happen. — A Post and Garrison is therefore established here which mounts 30 pieces of Cannon from 9 to 2 pounders but is only Calculated as a Secure retreat for the Europeans in case of an insurrection. The Troops now here are 30 under the Command of an Ensign. —

There are still some Portugueze on the Island and the Bastard Tribe are numerous under a Governor on the North side, but place called Daylie, but the accounts given to me of them afford no favorable Idea of him or the Country he resides at. — the whole settlement is frequently in want of food and sends here for Rice. — The place also is very unhealthy from a Want of Good fresh Water and a sufficiency of it, there is nevertheless Sandal Wood and Wax exported from thence, but in what quantities is not known. —

The Trade of the Dutch is here carried on by the Chinese who have many Vessels from 10 to 30 Tons burthen with which they sail to different Islands, and to the North and South side of this according to the Monsoon. As this Trade is carried on by barter it has and may be again very lucrative, for the Islands are numerous and European Articles are now in common use among the Malays who exchange principally Sandle Wood and Wax, of the latter they get a considerable quantity, the Bees building their Nests in the Bushes and Boughs of Trees. — The Vessels are Navigated by Malays so that it is only necessary for a Chinese to go as a Supercargo it is however necessary to be Well armed. —

Thus far only am I yet acquainted with the state of Timor. — The Dutch from former ties thought it proper to take the part of the lawfull Emperor, but altho the Governor had Troops from Batavia to more completely Garrison the Fort and sent Malay Troops to the Field yet the rebellion con=tinued for near three Years before the Emperor got the better of the Enemy. — who from supplication had a peace granted on certain conditions. —

As the Armies became numerous supplies of necessary food were less regular and almost a total Want followed. — Large parties then Marronid for themselves so that Cattle and Stock of every kind were wantonly destroyed, and a great scarcity was the consequence. — The indolence of the Malays render them unfit to speedely get the better of such a Disaster and is in part the Cause of the scarcity of Provisions which is at this time. —

The cultivation of Rice likewise is very inconsiderable from the natural indolence of the Natives, and Indian Corn which might be produced in large quantities is scarce to be got; but the latter is considered as an inferior Grain and used oßly by the lower Order of people, it is therefore not to be Wondered at that it is necessary for Supplies to be brought from Batavia. — As a Cause too, it may be owing to every one having a total indifference to Bread, for of that Article or Flour I am sure there is not 500 lw in the whole place. — Rice is their whole Support, and as they care for little else altho they cannot of themselves produce sufficient; it is not surprizing that they are often subject to Want. —

There is a kind of Market place formed by Slaves who sell Tobacco & Beetle Small Rice Cakes — Oranges Pompions — Sweet Potatoes — Scallions — Rape Greens — Plantains and a few other Articles. — But all these things are in such small quantities that a Man could carry the whole on his Shoulder. — Malay Countrymen also bring in Articles every day, but altho such a disposition to barter one would imagine would turn to some account yet I have seen a Man bring only two Potatoes to sell for which being bought for 2 Doits (equal to a halfpenny) has immidiatly laid them out in Beetle and lounged the remaining part of the day about the Town. — This is not a singular instance but gives the real Character of the Whole people as they appear to me and as I have them represented by People who professedly know them. —

As I doubted, and indeed was sensible that the Governors Ill health could seldom permit me to see him, I took this Opportunity to know if it would be agreeable to him to let Mr. Nelson examine the Country for Plants He most readily granted me the favor with an offer of every Assistance that I might stand in need of, and assured me that it was a country well worth examining and full of Medicinal Plants. — For Wounds a most efficacious application is by means of a Root of a Shrub or Small Tree. which being Scraped and applied mixt up with some Spirit never fails of a Speedy Cure. — Remarkable Cures have been performed with this Root. the property of which is said to be discovered by a Malay in the following Curious and singular Manner. —

In his Walk through the Woods he struck at a Snake that was lying in the Path and cut it in two but for a Small thread of the Skin. — The Creature as is common with them not to be immedeatly dispossessed of Life moved into the Bushes dragging its hinder part. untill it got to a particular Tree which the Malay observed him to lick with his tongue and alternately the amputated part. — Whether from design or Accident is a doubt, but on the day following the Man repassed the same Spot. and looking after the Snake found it perfectly joined and therefore brought it home with him to identify the fact. — From this circumstance the Root was taken up and has been very successfully applied. —

My intentions being to leave Timor as soon as possible, that I might be enabled to leave Batavia before the sickly Monsoon sets in, induced me to sollicit the Governor's assistance; as he joined with me in Opinion, that if I remained here untill the Vessels that were in the Road. were ready to Sail, I might not get to Batavia before the beginning of Nov.r and thereby lose the Opportunity of the Dutch Fleet that Sails in October for Europe. — in which Case I must remain untill January for our own China Ships that then pass through Streights Sunda, a length of time in the Sickly Season that I should avoid by every means in my power., I therefore determined to Hire or purchase a Vessel to carry me to Batavia, for I considered altho I had performed a much greater Voyage in my Boat, yet it would be unjustifiable to proceed in her any farther. — My Expences to Government. became also materially a cons of consideration, and it evidently appeared to me that the most effectual way to lessen such a burthen, was by adopting such means as would enable me to be the soonest in Europe: I no longer hesitated to purchase or Hire a Vessel. as I should find most elligible

Several Breadfruit which are by the Malays called. Sucoom were offered to sale this day. — I had one dressed. but it being a little decayed I could not consider it a proper sample of what may be got, it was notwithstanding very good and of the same Kind as at Otaheite, without seed. — The People here roast and eat them cut in slices with Milk and Sugar, but consider them of no value as bread kind. —

Remarks at Coupang Friday 26th June 1789. —

Light Winds Variable with Calms and Cloudy Weather. —
In general we are now recovering our strength very fast, so that I have every reason to to hope that we shall leave this hospitable place in perfect health. — Bathing in the River and Exercise is all that we now require except three of us who cannot keep free of Fever Mr Max the Doctor is however peculiarly attentive and has taken great pains and trouble. —

I took Mr Nelson with me to day to the Governors Gardens and found a Variety of fine Fruit Trees that we were not acquainted with but by Name. These were the Nanka or Sosac — Blimbing — Karangbola — Boabidarah — Syboah Jambolang and Jambo. —

The Nanka or Sosac, the latter being the Malay Name, is a very large fruit it grows from the Trunk of the Tree and not pendant from the Branches like most other fruit and when Ripe will Weigh from 10 to 20 lbs — the Rind is rough & prickly. — On being cut it is full of Seed which are coated with the eatable part of the fruit. — There are two kinds of this Fruit the Nanka Bobor, or Jack, and Nanka Salak. — I know no difference from the Outside, but on the inside one is more juicy and luscious than the other, the One the least so is however the highest flavoured, and the other resembles our Sour Sop in the West Indies to which the Rind also has a likeness. — The Seed is rather delicate but the Tree large. —

The Blimbing is a small acid fruit that grows from the body of the Tree as the Sosac does, altho not larger than a Common Girkin. — What one might have reasoned on from Nature in the Sosac, that the branches are subject to be borne down by the great Weight of the Fruit and therefore was Ordained should grow from the Trunk. is not applicable to the Blimbing. — it is used in Soops and as a Pickle. —

The Karangbola is a very pleasant fruit and very juicy, having something of the taste of Gooseberry before it is Ripe, with respect to the degree of acid in it. — It grows from 2 to 4 Inches long having five Edges, between which a finger may be laid, and when it is cut through the Middle it has the resemblance of a Star. — It is a small but pretty Tree. —

The Boabidarah and Jambolang were not in Season and only beginning to blossom

The Sybvah is a fruit produced from the Palm Tree, it is about the Size of a penny loaf and nearly round.——The Rind or Coat is somewhat similar to a Cocoa Nut, which covers three and sometimes only two Nutts full the size of a large Chesnut the shell is thin, and within it is a Whitish substance without Seed or pip not much unlike a Jelly but of a much firmer substance, the taste is pleasant tho' not remarkable.—

The Jambo is a plentifull Fruit and highly pleasant and gratefull to the taste, besides being the most refreshing.—Here are two kinds about the size of a common Apple—One has a dark red Skin and the other white tinged with red, the latter is most Juicy and is the same as the Otaheite Ayyah.—The Tree grows to a Moderate Size—The leaf like that of a Peach.—It has one kernel or Seed covered only by a Skin brown Skin and is difficult to keep.—

The Long Pepper or Seree Boah is here in abundance the Plant is a runner like our Scarlet Beans and the Fruit very like what is called the Plantains which is gathered out of the Fields in England to give to Linnets the leaf is somewhat formed like the Ace of Spades and constitutes a great part of the Beetle luxury as they could use no other part without it.—The Seree is either the leaf of the same plant or one of a like Nature, for we could see no difference Yet I am told the Seree does not bear the Seree Boah.

The Quid of Beetle is composed as follows—Two leaves of Seree have as much mixed lime called (Capore) put on them as can be taken up with the small end of a tea spoon which folded up is put into the Mouth, with about a quarter of the Peenang Nutt—about the size of a large Pea of a compound earth called Gambeir follows it, and being chewed for a Minute produceth a prodigious quantity of Saliva as red as blood.—After this they add a little Tobacco and bite occasion- ally of the Seree Boah as the Quid grows Weak.—People in general who use the Seree have their teeth jet black, but a few of the Ladies (for they all Chaw) who wish it have their teeth very white.—

Durions—Mungostains. Champadah—Lansa and Salac are not

to be found here. —

The Mangos were beginning to blossom. — Here are several kinds, but the Mango Dodole or Dodle is said to be the highest flavoured. — It is a large elegant growing Tree. —

We saw many Guava Trees and the Annonah or Custard Apple but the former had no fruit. —

Here are many Pomgranates and are nearly ripe — Pine Apples and Grape Vines close the Accounts of the Fruit that I am yet acquainted with, the former had no fruit and the latter will not bear untill December. —

The Kitchen Garden was ill Managed for there were but very indifferent Greens or even Sallad, altho. the Situation was on the Banks of the River. — Saw two Breadfruit Trees tolerably full of Fruit but they were stinted and shrivelled which I think was owing to the poor Spot of Ground they were in. —

Remarks at Coupang. from Saturday 27.th to Monday 29^h June 1789

Sultry W^r

     Some relapses have taken place, others however continue to gather Strength. but some with Sores in their Legs are troublesome to heal. — I still con= =tinue very Weak. —

     On the 27th I found the Suns Meridian Altitude of the Center to be 56..27 from whence by Old Tables for the Suns Declination I found the lat^e to be 10..12 S^o ~

     The Governors Ill health begins to render his life very precarious. I have nevertheless the greatest Attention from Mr Wanyon. —

     I have given publick Notice of my intentions to hire a Vessel to carry us to Batavia and have had several offers but none under 95 0 Dollars for simply the Papage, for they state the expence for 7 Months, as it will be that before the Vessel can return again on Account of the Monsoon. — In this point of view it is certainly preferable to purchase a Vessel. altho at present none Offer under 1200 Rix Dollars. —

     On Sunday performed Divine Service

<u>Remarks at Coupang 30th June and 1st July 1789 —</u>

Fine pleasant Wr and SE¼. Winds

Having now done my utmost by Publick enquiries and Notice to get a Vessel to proceed with the Officers and Men under my Command to Java at the lowest expence. On the 1st I thought it best for His Majestys Service to purchase one for 1000. Rix Dollars. — This was the lowest price I could get any one at that was safe to proceed to Sea in and that wanted so few Repairs — She was to be completed for Sea with Sails. Rigging and two Anchors and Cables the afsistance of my Carpenter included, I therefore directed her to be got to a proper place for repairing and my Carpenter to go to Work on the 3d following with some Chinese. and called her the Resource. —

		F	In
Her extreme Breadth on Deck		10	7
Do Length		34	7
Tred on the Ground		20	11
Depth in the Hold		5	0

Java Built. —

The 1st at Noon Meridian Altitude ☉ Center 56..41 from whence by Old Tables of Declination the latitude is 10..12 South. —

This day also I presented on Service to the Governor an Account of the lofs of my Ship and demanded in His Majestys Name that Orders might be sent to all their Settlements to take the Pirates if they came there. — A Complete description List was also given in. —

Fair Weather and ESE Winds. —

The symptoms of a perfect re-establishment of health from some unknown cause begin to fail among four of us who have intermitting Fevers but the rest are doing very well.. —

I find that it is so long back as the 20th April 1630 that the Dutch first made a Settlement of Coupang upwards of 159 Years, a series of time that one would imagined must have produced something remarkable. One cannot help therefore being Surprized at the few advantages which a set of Europeans have implanted among these people and at how little they have benefited the Country — Neither one or the other has certainly ever been even a secondary con= =sideration with them, for if we were to take Coupang away we should discover no Signs (if we except a few descendants,) of their having been here, to the honor or Credit of their establishment. — As far as absolute necessity or convenience led them to Marry, their progeny became an improvement (as it may be called for I do not think so myself) if the Malay Reading and Writing was inculcated and those few were benefitted. Even this degree of improvement one would have imagined must have been dispersed to marry by this time, and that it would have spread itself about the Country at least near to Coupang, but on the contrary no Marks of it are to be found but in the Town. where the Malay connection with the Dutch seems so totally seems forgot their Original that there does not appear to be one single natural tye of Blood between them and the Country people —

By the long connection however of the Dutch with the Malays they have acquired a perfect Knowledge of their language and have reduced it to Grammar, by which Means they have had the Scriptures translated and the prayers at Church are always in the Evening service performed in that tongue. —

The Malays in general are a well proportioned set of People, and to a person acquainted he cannot hesitate a Moment to believe that the South Sea Islanders and them are of the same Origin. — Among the real Malays that are those who are not connected with the Dutch) will be found a great similarity of language and no doubt customs — of the latter I observe the Tuggee tuggee of the Friendly Islands which they call Toombock and the Hoomee of Otaheite which they call Ramas. — They Count Ten as follows — Osa — Roah — Tainoo. — Ha. — Neemah — Nai — Heetoo — Seeoha — Sannaoolu. — These numbers bear a great Similarity — They call Fish Eeka — the Eyes Mattah and Mattee Signifies dead or Killed. —

   I cannot discover that any kind of Spice is cultivated in this Island on the contrary I am assured it is the Companys express commands that it is rooted out wherever it is found. —

   Among the Curiosities of this place are found the Eatable Birds Nest. — Of this article a private Trade is carried on, but as the quantity that is found is but small, it can be of no valuable consideration altho the price appears to make up for the Scarcity They are sold here at 13 Rix Dollars pr lb. and at Java for 15 or 20 pr lb. — I cannot get a Knowledge with certainty of what kind of Bird it is that makes this Nest, but from some Malay Mens account it is of a Species of the Swallow like the Mother Careys Chicken. — They build in the Rocks and near to the Sea, for according to description the Malays are obliged frequently to dive under the Water to get up into the Caverns and Holes into which there is no acces from without, and it is certain they have a great deal of difficulty and trouble in getting them. —

   A Cockle shell about 3 Inches long is about the Size and form of these Nests which are made or wove by threads of glutinous matter that no one has an Idea how it is collected. — Whiteness constitutes a great part of the Value of this Article. — Its principal virtues is strengthening and nourishing the Stomach, I never heard however that it is ever dressed alone — they always add a Fowl, and the broth then appears to be Chicken with Vermacelli mixt with it and to the Palate not better. — In China they are highly Valued One Nest disolved in a large Tea Cup of boiling Water or nearly to that proportion and drank in the Mornings is considered very advantageous to Weak constitutions —

Remarks at Coupang, Friday 3rd to Sunday 5th July 1789. —

Fine W. and fresh ESE. Winds: —

On the 3d I ordered the Carpenter to Work on board His Majesty's Schooner Resource.

Our health is yet not reestablished – Four are ill with intermitting Fevers and myself subject to a great straitness across my breast. – Bathing in the River before sun rise and walking in the cool of the day is the only remedy for the Convalescents. – Our Walks are confined to within 2 and 4 Miles round the Neighbourhood. — In this Circuit Old Stone Walls and Fences are numerous and many Ruinaters which seem to point out that at some distant period back this was a place better Cultivated and more thickly inhabited. – The Roads are very stoney and the land every where covered with Brush Wood. – Perhaps the finest Tamarind Trees in the World are to be found here. – Every person if they have but a Yard of Ground. Cultivate a few Plants of Tobacco they however from not knowing how to Manufactor it, produce only a very poor Commodity Gardening is the most neglected here that I ever saw it where any Europeans had been, a good Cabbage or bunch of Greens is not to be got. —

Remarks at Coupang Monday 6th July 1789. –

Fair Weather and SEg Winds. –

     My Carpenter and Chinese to work about the Vessel. – Boatswain

Employed about the Rigging and Sailmakers about the Sails. –

Remarks at Coupang. Tuesday 7th July 1789. —

Fair W. and Moderate E.S.E. Winds. Employed about the Vessel.

Mr. Wanjon whose utmost Study and Endeavors are to render my situation at Coupang agreeable requested of me to spend the day with him at Owar. — Mr. Nelson accompanied us and found many Curious Plants but defered collecting as he expects a Week longer would be vastly advantageous. —

The Slaves were principally employed preparing the Cocoa Nutts for making Oil — Four Nutts will make near a Pint. — The process is by Scraping the Old Nutts down and putting it into a Vessel over a Slow Fire untill the Oil is produced. — it is then fit for any of the Uses to which Sweet Oil is applied —

We saw the Rattah or Otaheite Chesnutt here but no Fruit on the Trees the Malay Name for it is Gàigh. — Saw many of those Curious Trees which throw out Roots from the Branches and Striking down into the Ground become large Trunks of themselves and surrounding the Parent Tree and sometimes connecting with it form large Congeries of Trunks curious to behold. — These Trees grow to a Considerable height, but Mr. Wanjon told us that in the Island Samow they exceed all imagination the Branches spreading many hundred Yards in Circumference. —

A very destructive Ant is here which destroys Trees and Dwellings in a very short time if not observed It is very little bigger than the common black Ant its head is yellow and body light Coloured. —

A Small kind of Paroquet are innumerable here and fine Wood Pigeons Wild Ducks are also plenty. —

Mrs. Wanjon favored us with her Company and a Dinner was prepared with all the dainties of Timor among which were very fine Carp. —

Robt. Tinkler the Masters Brother in Law, having behaved Saucy & impertinent to the Boatswain, received some little chastisement for it. upon which it appears the Master interfered and Order'd him to stick his Knife into the Boatswain As soon as I became acquainted with this matter, I as publickly reprimanded the Master, making him responsible & equally Criminal with Tinkler in case any such Violence is committed. —

Remarks at Coupang Wednesday 8th to Thursday 9th July 1789.

Fresh Easterly Winds and Fair Wr. Empd. about the Sails & Rigging of the Resource. —

A Chinese Prow about 20 Tons came in about ⅔ loaded with Sandle Wood and Wax for which they barter with Iron Work and Fire Arms. — As I have already mentioned, the Bees build their Nests in the Branches of Trees or Bushes to which the Natives cannot approach but by Fire so that the Swarms are Numerous that they destroy. — The Honey is put into Jars and the Wax is run into Blocks that are about 3 feet long and a foot or 15 Inches Square. —

Mr. Nelson imprudently leaving off some Warm Cloathing caught cold and had an Attack of a Fever. —

Remarks at Coupang Friday 10th to Monday 13th July 1789.

Fresh Breezes Easterly and Fair Wr.

Mr. Nelson continues very Ill – He is most carefully attended by Mr. Max and Mr. Ledward our own Surgeon. –

On the 10th the Carpenter taken ill of a Fever. – Chinese at Work about the Schooner but go on exceedingly slow. –

On Sunday I performed Divine Service in the Morning, and in the Afternoon I went to Church where the Service was performed by a Malay. The Congregation were nearly 50 persons most of whom were Malays. –

This little place of Coupang is governed by an Opperhooft and Raad, which is a Governor and Council. – The Council consists of the Second Governor or Secunde as he is called. – The Doctor – Secretary and Officer of the Troops. – Before them all cases are tryed but things of a Criminal nature are determined at Batavia. – Their Courts are held in the Castle where are also the Companys Stores – Hospital and Barracks. –

Remarks at Coupang Tuesday 14th July 1789. —

Fair Weather and fresh Breezes at ESE. — Employed on the Schooner. —
Mr. Nelson very Ill and most dilligently attended by Mr. Max and his Assistant, also
Mr. Bertz and our own Surgeon. — They use no Purgatives but frequent.

Carpenter getting better. — Three others have intermitting Fevers. — Myself much
recovered but very Weak. —

This Morning I attended a Chinese Funeral the Person was
of the superior Class at this place the Order of the Funeral was said therefore to be
attended with suitable Pomp and grandeur. —

Old Age with its usual infirmities caused the death of this Man, and
as the approaches were regular, he had directed and got his Coffin made at an
early period, which I am told he often looked at with great composure neither
showing a desire or a dread of Death — Life therefore about which we have
so much solicitude and anxious care appeared only a secondary consideration
with him, so that he had arrived at that State of present happiness altho
a real Idolator, which is the grand Object with every good Christian. —

The Body lay four days, the Third it was put into the Coffin and the
Necessary preparations for the Funeral were completed. —

On the 4th day at 4 in the Morning the ceremony began by a Clattering
of Metal Pans (called Gongs) two small Trumpets and two Flutes — With the latter
at intervals they played a dirge, and the Gongs at every quarter of an hour were
beat with great Violence for the space of a Minute. — The Men relations of the deceased
were dressed in White Callico Habits made as their common habiliments are, and
the Women had Veils of the same Cloth. — Two Boys dressed as the Men each with a
piece of Bamboo two feet long performed the Office of Mutes. — The Coffin was
painted black ornamented with gilded Characters and an Iron Skewer went
down past the left Shoulder to the bottom of the Coffin. — The procession was in
pairs the first held large paper Lanthorns with a Candle lighted in each carried
at the top of long Poles which raised them 8 or 10 feet above the Ground. — Next was

carried a Hoop covered with Red Satten like a Petticoat. — Then followed by Pairs about 2 dozen decorative Paper Ensigns and One of Red Satten. A Sedan Chair, with a Small pot put therein filled with Sand in which was stuck a Number of small Sticks covered with some Composition which made them burn without Blaze, closed the Order while the Corps was got ready to be removed out of the House upon the Bier. —

In the Room where the Corps lay was a Table spread with some Tea Equipage — At the back of it was a Kind of Paper Altar with Chinese Characters, and underneath a Pot of burning small Sticks and Candles on each Side. — Adjoining was another Table spread with dressed Fowls Ducks a Leg of Pork and part of Harslet. — On the left of the Altar was a Goat cleaned of its Hair fixed on a bier for that purpose, in the attitude of listening or Alarmed at some Sounds that it heard; and on the Right was Hog in a similar position

The two Brothers of the deceased with his Son stood before the Altar at the end of the Tables — One Man stood on the left and two on the Right of them to perform the Office of Priests and one of them kneeling down read a prayer. — After the Prayer a Cup of Tea, or what was in the Tea pott was presented on a Silver Waiter to the middle Person seven different times, who after paying a Devotion to the Altar and Manes of the deceased returned it to the Altar. A Basket of Gilded papers were set fire to before the door to which also they paid Devotion. — One of the Brothers kneeled down by the side of the Coffin and appeared to be in conversation with the deceased, when one of my Seamen swore he was bespeaking a good birth for himself in the Next World. which if he had permitted me to have had my own Ideas on it. I should have asked, if one might have reasoned from this, that their happiness in a future State is in their Idea in some degree procured by the intercessions of their Friends who die before them —

But the expression of the Seaman is as emphatical and no one can deny but it is more concise. —

The Slaves and Servants took their farewell of their Master by loud shouts of Grief The Victuals were removed from the Table into a Basket, and the Hog and Goat were taken into an adjoining House. — The Corps was now taken out on a Bier during which the Symbols made a great Noise as if to overcome the Grief that takes place on the removal of the Body. —

The Altar also was removed out and carried before the Corps, and the procession moved off with their Friends and acquaintance following in Pairs and after all the Female Mourners. — Three Swivels were fired and Rockets at every 5 Minutes and the Road was strewed with gilded papers as they went to the Grave where the Body was deposited with no other ceremony than each person throwing a handfull of Earth on the Coffin, the Female Mourners walking three times round the Grave, and a Bundle of Gilded papers burnt as they had done before the House. —

The Men remained to see the Grave closed during which the Victuals were spread on the Ground and the Altar held at the Grave and any person that chose eat or drank. — Some devotions were then performed by the two Brothers by bowing and Kneeling, after which the Victuals were taken up and every one returned Home. —

Remarks at Coupang. Wednesday 15th. and Thursday 16th July 1789 –

Fresh Breezes. and Fair Wr. with light Winds at Night. – Wind ESE

Mr Nelson very ill. – Three Invalids. – Carpenter returned to his duty on the 15th – Employed about the Vessel.

As I have expressed a desire to see the Seed Breadfruit Mr Wanjon had some sent from the Country to shew me. – If we except colour this Fruit has no resemblance to the other. – Its surface is covered with projecting points near an half Inch long which give it the Appearance of being covered with prickles but these points are tender and being easily broke emitts a Milky substance like the other fruit but its inside is full of large seed which may be compared to Windsor Beans and are equally good when either boiled or Roasted. – No other part is eatable. – The Tree I am told is to all appearance the same as that which bears the Fruit without Seed. or the Otaheite kind and is called Succoom Raja, the other Succoom Beijee. – I proposed to Mr Nelson before his Illness to take some of the good kind away with us. but if a change does not shortly take place in his Illness I am very apprehensive I shall have the misfortune to lose him –

Remarks Friday 17th July 1789

D°. W°. — Employed about the Vessel — Every assistance is given to M.r Nelson but he remains extremely ill. —

I got the following account to day of the time the Dutch made their Settlements among these Islands. —

January 1.st — 1601 — Ternate conquered.
" 14.th — 1644 — Malacca D°.
February 23.° – 1605 – Ambon D°
April :26.th – 1630 — Coupang in Timor D°.
July – 2.nd — 1609 — Began Trade with Japan
15.th — 1664 — Macassar conquered.
August 13.th — 1609 — Banda. D°.
July 15.th — 1662 – Malabar D°.
May – 30.th — 1619 – Batavia – D°.
April 6.th — 1652. Cape Good Hope settled. —

Also their Geographical situation of Places counting the first Meridian from the Pic of Tenariff. —

Place		Lat.	Long.
Cape of Good Hope		33..55 S.°	34 .. 36 E
Amboina – Casteel Victoria		3.. 40	145 .. 55
Banda — Casteel Belgica		4.. 35	147.. 20
Ternaten — Casteel Oranje		0.. 45 N.°	144 .. 00
Macassar — Casteel Rotterdam		5.. 00 S.°	136.. 50
Banjer in Borneo		2.. 40	131.. 40
Pontiana in D°.		0.. 30	135.. 30
Timor — — Casteel Concordia		10.. 11	138.. 20
Palembang in Sumatra		2.. 40	120.. 3
Padang in D°.		0.. 45	116.. 5
Japan — Nangasaki		33. 00 N.°	140. 40
Malacca — Casteel Malacca		3. 10	140. 45
Coromandel – Negapatnam		10.. 40	95.. 40
Ceylon — Colombo		7.. 00	95.. 30

Mallabar —	op Cochin	6..50 N°	92..00 E'
Souratte —		21..10	80..00
Java —	op Samaran	6..55 S°	127..30
Cheribon	Casteel de Bescherming	6..50	124..15
Bantam	Casteel Speelwyck	6..5	121..20
Batavia	Casteel Diamans	6..10	122..17

Several Prows have arrived this Week loaded with Sandle Wood and Bees Wax. which was all landed at the Chinese Stores — These industrious and busy people have a part of the Town allotted to them that is next to the Sea Side and is called the Camp. — They are under a Captain and are quiet and good Citizens — almost all the Vessels belong to them and through these People all the Trade of this place is carried on. ——

Remarks at Coupang Saturday 18th to Monday 20th July 1789.

Fresh Gales at ESE and Fair Wr. Moderating towards Night. — Employed on board the Vessel. —

At ½ past One on Monday Afternoon Mr David Nelson departed this life — The Fever was inflamatory. — This loss of this Honest Man bears very heavy on my mind. — his duty and integrity went hand in hand, and he had accomplished through great care and diligence the object he was sent for; always forwarding every plan I had for the good of the Service we were on. — He was equally serviceable in my Voyage here in the Course of which he always gave me pleasure by Conducting himself with Resolution and integrity. —

Remarks at Coupang. Tuesday 21st and Wednesday 22nd July 1789.

Fresh Winds at ESE and fair Wr. Employed Caulking and other duties on board the Resource. —

On the 21st. I was employed regulating the Funeral of Mr. Nelson, — The Order of which was as follows. — At 5 OClock the Corps carried by 12 Soldiers in black preceded by the Minister. — Next followed myself and Second Governor then ten Gentlemen of the Town and Officers of the Ships and after them my own Officers and People. —

After reading our burial Service the Body was interred behind the Chappel in the Ground appropriated to the Europeans of the Town

I was sorry to find I could get no Tomb Stone at this place, that a stranger might have Contemplated that a Man lay there who had surmounted every Calamity and distress for eight and forty days across a dangerous Sea with Fortitude and health; but that at last after surmounting every difficulty, and in the midst of his humble gratitude and joy to Almighty God for his preservation; he paid this debt which human Weakness would have believed was to have been at a more distant period. —

On Wednesday Prayers were performed at the Chappel for the Recovery of the Governor who now lies dangerously Ill. —

Remarks at Coupang Thursday 23rd July 1789.

Fresh Gales ESE. and SE, Fair Wr. Employed about the Vessel. —

Our health is now tolerably reestablished. there are however still two Invalids. —

Besides the River Water, here are some Charming Springs, so that the former is scarce ever used but for the purposes of cleaning. — To bring the Water to the house. they have Buckets made from the leaves of the Palm Trees which hold 3 & 4 Gallons — These Trees are in great abundance all over the Country, and at a distance resemble the Cocoa Nutt. — From the likeness of the leaf to a Fan they are called the Fan Palm. They are Valuable from producing a Clear liquor called Toack which is an agreeable and Wholesome drink, and when boiled produceth a very rich Syrup of the consistency of Treacle that if properly fined is a very good Sweetner. — The Island Sabou is a noted place for this Syrup and Vessels come here from that place with great quantities for Sale. — We gave for a Jar that held about 3 Gallons 30 Stivers but the Inhabitants get it for half the price. ——

The liquor is got by cutting a Notch in the Branches to which they hang a bucket to receive the Juice and is called tapping the Tree. — They bear the Fruit I have described under the Name of Syboah. ——

The amount of my enquiries respecting the Weather and Monsoons at this Island are thus. — That the Companys ships are not allowed to lye in the Road (which is Open from the North to WNW.) before the 16th March the Next Monsoon being then considered to be nearly Over. — April the Easterly Wind or Monsoon begins but the Weather is sometimes Variable untill May when the Easterly Wind is Steady and blows so untill October when it becomes Variable again with Rain and Westerly Winds which are fixed in the Month of December. ——

These changes in some degree reach as far as Otaheite, with this difference that the Westerly Winds do not blow so constant, but in other respects alike. — The Summer Solstice is the general time of the Change. —

Very Fresh Gales Easterly and fair Wr. People in general are troubled with Colds and say these strong Winds are very unhealthy it is therefore not surprizing that I have still two Invalids. —

Carpenters Employed about the Vessel, but such bad Workmen that it goes very slowly on. — On the 25th. I finished my Observations on the Tides. —

At full and Change it is high Water. 11 OClock in the forenoon and the Rise of the Tide is 8 feet 8 Inches, but on the height of the Springs it rises about 9 feet 6 Inches and it is high Water then at ¾ past Noon or One OClock according to the Winds

I saw a Lucus Naturæ to day a Malay Woman who had White Hair, Eye brows and Eye lashes, was exceedingly near Sighted and her Skin White, but very rough and much freckled. Her Eyes were Grey. —

On Sunday performed Divine Service. —

We continue bathing every Morning in the River at a place of the Governors called Montassy which has restored the most of us to our Usual Strength but my Sick list is now encreased by a third person and all of them intermitting Fevers. —

Remarks at Coupang Wednesday 29th July 1789. —

Light Northerly Winds — Three Men ill with intermitting Fevers. Mr. Max the Town Doctor attending Constantly. — Mr. Ledward our Own Surgeon being One of the Sick. — Every proper Article is got for them that is necessary. —

The Residence of the Emperor or Keyser as he is called, is at Backennassy a pretty place about 4 Miles from Town — By appointment I paid him a Visit to day for I was particularly desirous to see him as he was the person whose Nephew had caused the War that was in the Island a Short time since. —

The Situation of Backennassy is very pleasant and airy with a pretty View of the Sea — The River which empties itself at Coupang runs through it, so that it is Charmingly Watered and produces a large Quantity of Rice. The Country is exceedingly picturesque, but the Hills in general are very rocky and scarce soil sufficient to produce Grass in the Rainy Season. — I imagine I saw about 150 Acres of Rice, and in some places the Harvest is begun. — About this part of the Country it is charmingly cloathed with Cocoa Nutts and other Trees. — The Cocoa Nutts and other Trees — are very fine, and the Trees I think bear greater quantities than in the South Sea. — Plantains are also in great perfection and the Sugar Cane grows luxuriantly, but I cannot find that the latter is for any other use than eating, to which I attribute that only small quantities are to be met with.

The Bread fruit Tree which is a Native of this Island as much as it is of Otaheite, grows with great luxuriance — I saw about 20 Trees some of which were larger than I ever saw at Otaheite. — They produce identically the same Fruit; but from what cause I know not the Fruit is not so good. — Equal sized fruit would weigh nearly one half heavier at Otaheite. — It must certainly be owing to the Soil — They are nevertheless very good and I have had several dressed since I have been at Coupang. — The Natives eat them with milk. —

This being the Height of the dry Season the Ground is scorched up in every place, so that not a blade of Grass is to be seen, it therefore is the cause that the Cattle are exceedingly Poor for they have nothing to feed on but leaves. — The few sheep that are about the neighbourhood of Coupang are small and so are the horned Cattle except the Karabows or Wild Ox. —

The Horses are likewise small. but are pleasant travelling Animals and are sure footed. — Goats thrive here very well. — Hogs are very scarce, and as Indian Corn is but thinly planted the Poultry is as poor as at any Island in the South Sea, unless they are particularly fed. —

There is nothing merits my mentioning the reception I met with from the Emperor but his Civility. — I found him to be an Elderly Man. — His dress was a Cheque Wrapper girded round his Waist by a Silk and Gold Belt. a loose linnen Jacket and a Coarse Handkerchief about his Head. — His dwelling was the Shell of a large House, which was only divided into three Apartments surrounded by a Piazza — It was well situated but very dirty, and the few Chairs and Tables that he had. were in the same State. — About a pint of Arrack was all he had, that however was the first thing he offered to me besides the Bettle. — A few Chief Malays were with him, and after making some enquiries who I was and how I came to the Island; Tea was set before me with some Rice Cakes made up and fryed with Cocoa Nutt Oil. some Toasted Indian Corn and two Saucers of dryed Buffaloe Flesh. —

The Curiosities in this Repast were the two last Articles. The Indian Corn by the Mode of drying it turned the Grains inside out and perhaps is the most tempting pretty Dish that can be put on a Table. as a Desert altho' a great deception. — The Manner of drying it is this. — An Iron Pan is put over the fire into which a Spoonfull of some oily substance is put — as soon as it becomes hot, about a large handfull of Corn is put therein and kept stirring untill it has imbibed all the fat — the heat of the Pan having then nothing else to Act upon but the Corn, every Grain begins to burst and fly about for which you are prepared with a Cover which is laid on untill the Cracking is over when the whole is taken out. —

The Buffalo Flesh is so dryed that it is beat to thread and dust before it can be used — it is however very palatable, and might be eat on bread and Butter as well as Parmesan Cheese. —

The repast was no sooner over than the Emperor with three of the Chiefs who had partook of it retired and after a short deliberation they came out and presented to me a round Metal piece (4 Inches Diameter with a Star stampt on it,) as a present which of Course I readily accepted, a mutual compliment of bowing passed between us, and he appeared highly pleased that I could thank him in the Malay language.

As I knew liquor was of great Value among these people I was prepared to make my present, and I found the Arrack which I had brought for the purpose to be highly acceptable. —

As indolence forms a great part of the Character of the Malays so the Beetle is admirably well calculated to Gossip away their time, it is always the first thing presented and laying aside the Tobacco it may be used without much disgust by any European whatever. — No one dilutes any liquor, every kind of Spirit is therefore drank in its real State, and habit has brought them to bear a large quantity at a time without being intoxicated. —

As I desired to take a Walk the Chiefs attended me, and I saw the Breadfruit already described. — The only new Fruit I met with was the Chermaila it is of a very agreeable tartness and acquires a Sweetness when Ripe grows in clusters from the Main Wood of the Branches - is about the size of a common Gooseberry and is very fine for all the purposes of that fruit - The Tree is about 15 feet high. — I saw a few Guava Trees with some Fruit on them. — the Malay name is Gooyavas - the Sugar Cane they Call Taboo. —

To make the Trees in general bear fruit they Chop the Trunk full of Cuts just as deep as to get through the Rind. — The Otahiteans point a piece of hard Wood a foot long and an Inch Diameter, and drive it into the body of their Bread fruit Trees to acquire the same End. —

On the Death of an Emperor large Feasts are made to which the whole inhabitants are supposed to be invited. — After a few days the Body is put into a Coffin or long Box closely shut up and is kept for 3 Years before the interment takes place. —

Since the Conquest the Dutch have endeavoured to establish Christianity this Emperor was therefore Christened Barnardus, his Malay Name being Bacchee bannock, but I cannot help observing that it has gained little other ground. in this Country except in the Town of Coupang. —

The Island might be Valuable to the Dutch was it solely under their jurisdiction, but the Portugeze settlements in the North causes a great division among the Malays., it is therefore the Case that what Trade might center at Coupang is carried off to the Portugese. — The Emperor himself declares that Gold dust used to be a part of their Traffic, but even Bees Wax and Sandal Wood would be Sufficient. from the latter an Oil of a very high perfume is extracted. —

The Indian or Natural Malay Houses are some times built round and at others in the common Way — Bamboos form generally the Side and partitions and the Roofs are thatched. — They are fond of Stone Fences which they make with little Trouble — The Villages and every ones property is on that Account marked out having a Wall round them. but as they use no Mortar they are more or less always in disorder. — From these kind of Fences which are now desolate here are many proofs of its having been a more populous Country than I now find it. —

The Malays have not that Cleanliness about them as is among the Natives of the Society and Friendly Islands, and owing to a want of it they are subject to the Itch. —

Their connections with the Europeans have given them the Itch Pox, and whenever it befals them it is attended with the most Cala=mitous circumstances sweeping off Vast numbers and desolating the Country. — Other disadvantages they seem to labour under from this intercourse, they appear not to have that life and Spirit which is the Native character of these Indians — I even observed a vast difference between our friends here and the more independant Malays who live under their own Cheifs far back in the Island. Many of whom I have seen in Town on their own business who possessed the quickness and power of a Freindly Islander. —

These People however have been taught mildness in their punishments, for in these Villages I have seen Offenders put into the Stocks the same as in Europe. — but the use no Irons altho Coupang rings with leg ornaments on miserable run aways and others who have behaved ill. —

I eat part of a Nanka to day that weighed 20 lbs — it was very delicious and high flavored — the seed also were exceedingly good when roasted. —

Remarks at Coupang Thursday 30th & Friday 31st July 1789 —

Light Winds NW'y. and Fair Wr. with East'y Winds at Night. —

Employed about the Vessel. — three Men in the Sick list with intermitting Fevers. —

About a dozen China Vessels have Sailed out of the River this Week and are gone to Trade for Sandle Wood and Wax. —

The Mango Trees are now in blossom and some of the Jambo= lang, and the Bushes in general indicate the advance of Spring — All these circumstances recalls to me the loss of Mr. Nelson. and the object of my Voyage, which at times almost bear me down, but for the impropriety to let so much Weakness get the better of me. —

I have forgot to mention a Fruit that is called Nam.nam — it is fit for any of the Uses we put the Apples to, such as Pyes &c.ª and has a large Seed that Vegetates very quickly as does the seed of the Nanka — It is a flat semicircular Fruit about 3 Inches long. —

Remarks at Coupang Saturday 1st August 1789.

Light Variable Winds and Fair Wr. Employed about the Vessel. — Two men in the Sick list — The Governor continues very ill. — Mr Wanjon continues to be peculiarly attentive to every thing I express a Desire to have done, and furnishes the Chinese with Material Articles to enable them to complete our little Vessel for Sea. —

I took a Ride to day into the Country to a View of the Governors called Oloomee about 8 Miles from hence, in the Course of which I took a Circuit of about 24 Miles I found in general any part of the high grounds very Rocky. and to produce nothing but Trees and Bushes which seemed equally to Suffer by the extreme heat and want of Rain to the Soil itself which was so burnt. that nothing appeared to be growing. — The Valleys and lower Grounds however were very different, these Parts were well Watered, the Trees grew luxuriantly, particularly the Cocoa Nutt and I had many beautifull Views of extensive Plantations of Rice. of these there one is called Laidamatta about 4 Miles from Coupang. —

The only Trees I was acquainted with that I saw growing and to be considered Natives, for I presume they never had been planted or touched by the hand of Man, was the Anona or Custard Apple. and the Sosac or Nanka, also the Tamarind. — The Cocoa Nutt I imagine is always allowed to be a Native of the Climate — With respect to those which appeared to me as extraordinary and curious I saw only one Kind. — They were very large Trees and at a little distance appeared to have lost the Rind and the milk white Trunk and branches indicated they had no life — but the senses are very agreeably surprized to find the Tree in full Vigor and the most beautifull Glossy White Sattin the natural appearance of the Bark. —

I crossed one very large River. the Water was low at this time, but there were evident proofs of great Torrents passing through in the Rainy Season. Many branches lead off from this River and the Lower Grounds are well Watered. —

Oloomee is in a pleasant Valley where the Governor keeps two Dutchmen to look after his Cattle Poultry and Hogs, who with a dozen Malays are the whole of the Inhabitants. — several Malay Settlements are within a few Miles of each other but a half dozen Houses is the largest I met with

Except the Valleys as I have mentioned before, the Country is very barren and good for Nothing — The Rainy Season may produce a little Grass, but during the Rest of the Year the Country is burnt up and but for the Bushes one would only see perforated Rocks and Stones which are equally Offensive to the Ear from a horrid jingling Sound they have as one Rides or Walks among them. —

The only Cattle I saw was the Karabow or wild Ox and some Goats. — The Karabow is the only Cattle of the Ox Kind that the Malays have — They are very poor and coarse eating. — The Country appears to me to be very thinly inhabited. — It was the middle of Harvest, yet I did not see about any one property above 6 persons and what was extraordinary, the Way they took in their Grain was by each person carrying a basket and striping the Ears off by hand. —

This day I applied to the Governor and Raad to be supplied with Cash for His Majestys Service and Engaged to give Bills on Government to the Amount. —

Remarks at Coupang Sunday 2nd to Wednesday 5th 1789. ——

Very Fresh Gales East Southy and Fair Weather — Two Men in the Sick List Intermitting Fevers —— Employed about the Vessel — On the 4th My Carpenter finished laying the Deck which has been 27 Days in doing — 5th Masted the Vessel. ——

A Chinese Prow came in loaded with Wax and Sandle Wood which was all landed at their own Stores. ——

I had some New Fruit procured for me to day called Sow — It is about the size and like a Red Plumb has a pleasant sweet taste and mealy like a Potatoe it had four Stone Seeds. ——

Remarks at Coupang Thursday 6th to Friday 8th August 1789

Fresh Breezes and Fair Wr. Wind ESE —

Employed Rigging and Fitting the Vessel. Sick List four Men intermitting Fevers — I have observed that those people who have been attacked with
the Fever have all been Swelled and bloated about the Face. — Bleeding was
Practised in the beginning —

I am now detained by the Governors Ill health — he is now
incapable of Speaking and is hourly expected to die. The Road therefore
cannot issue me any Supplies. —

Remarks at Coupang Sunday 9th to Tuesday 11th August 1789 —

Strong Breezes at ESE and Fair Wr. Variable Winds at Night. —
Four Men Ill with intermitting Fevers. —

On applying for Fire Wood Mr Wanjon immediately sent off a party of Malays to Cut the quantity I wanted. — Ballasted the Vessel and received five Puncheons of Water on board. On the 10th Received 2 Puncheons of Salt Meat One Containing 254 lbs Beef and the other 250 lbs Pork. —

On the 11th Received 504 lbs Rice in Bags. —
The Governor lying in a dying State Mr Wanjon most readily took the whole at his own Risk and will supply me with Cash and every thing I am in need of out of his own private fortune. —

Remarks at Coupang Wednesday and Thursday 12.th & 13.th August 1789

Fresh Breezes ESE moderating towards Night — Sick List three Men Still ill with intermitting Fever. —

12th I received 32 Gall.^s Arrack 5 lbs Sugar & 3 Gallons of Vinegar. —

As our Voyage to Java is subject to Accident from Piratical Vessels Mr Wanjon granted that I should have as a loan to be returned at Batavia the following Arms. —

Swivels Brass

1	H	192 lbs	Powder 50 lbs
2	&C	190	Flints - 42 in N.^o
3	V	195	Musq.^t Balls 560
4	A V&C	165	Musquetts - 14
			Bayonetts — 14
			Swivel Balls - 100
			Powder Horns - 2
			Priming Wires - 2

The above I gave the Gunner an Order to take in his Charge dated the 12th. —

The Piratical Vessels that infest these Seas are the People from Borneo and Celebes —

On the 13th I received 30 fine Plants that the Governor on my first Arrival from a request I made to him promised should be got ready for me I received others also from Mr Wanjon the whole consisting of Karang bolas - Jambos Nankas - Bread fruit Churmailan and others of a Fine Tree that bears leaves of a high perfume called Boong at Kanang at Mr Wanjon also got me some Seeds for His Majestys Garden at Kew. — The Breadfruit had but very little Roots I therefore think they may fail

Remarks at Coupang. Friday 14th to Tuesday 18th August 1789. —

Fresh Breezes Easterly and Fair Wr. — Three People Ill with intermitting Fever
The Secretary of the Company brought me in an Account a Tax of 5 pr Cent
on the Purchase of the Schooner; but I refused to pay any such Tax and it
was therefore laid on the Seller. —

        The Governor exists but that is all. — I am now busyly
employed. writing my letters. and getting my Accounts in a train for
settling. —

Remarks at Coupang. 19th and 20th August 1789.

Fresh Breezes Easterly and Fair Wr.—

Wednesday 19th I now closed all my Accounts both for Victualling and every other nature and gave Bills on His Majestys Navy and Victualling Boards

I left Letters to the Lords of the Admiralty and Navy and Victualling Board to be sent by the first ship that sailed.—

On the 20th in Forenoon I embarked and prepared to Sail.— I left the Governor at the Point of Death.— To this Gentleman is most our most grateful thanks for the humane and friendly treatment that we have received from him, and whose miserable State of health only prevented him from showing me more particular Marks of his attention. Unhappily it is to his Memory only that I now pay this poor Tribute— But it was a fortunate circumstance that the Secunde Mr. Wanjon was equally susceptible and ready to relieve us. His attention was unremitting, and more than all when there was a doubt about supplying me with money on Government Account to enable me to purchase a Vessel to proceed on my Voyage, he cheerfully took it upon himself without which it was evident I should be too late at Batavia to sail for Europe with the Fleet on the last of October.— I can only return such Services by Mentioning them to the Lords Commissioners of the Admiralty that if it may appear to their Lordships worthy of their Attention Mr. Wanjon may receive such promotion as to know his Zeal to assist His Majestys subjects has not been forgot.—

Mr. Max the Surgeon has attended us with the utmost care, for which I could not get him to render in any Account or answer, than that it was his Duty and would receive no Payment.—

In the Afternoon I sailed and was Saluted by the Shipping which I returned— At this Day at Noon Log Account begins being 12 Hours earlier than Civil Account of time according to which my Diary at Coupang has been kept—

I shall close my account with a few remarks I have omitted to mention among my common occurrences. —

The Town of Coupang is situated about 12 Miles to the NE of the SW point of Timor and in the SW part of a Great Bay where is a most excellent Road for Shipping The Town consists of about 150 Houses including Malays & Chinese. — Its situation is perhaps peculiarly desireable on Account of the Road and a fine River, and to the latter we may without Error attribute the great share of health that the Inhabitants enjoy. — It is also very advantageous to their Trade as it can admitt Vessels of 6 feet draught of Water. —

The European Houses are built of Stone with large Piazzas which with fine Trees branching over them The Whole of the dwelling is Cool and agreeable The River divides the Town — the Chinese Houses are along the Sea Shore and the Fort is on a Small emminence on the West side of the Rivers Mouth across which is a Bar of Sand. —

Along the Banks of the River grow very fine shady Trees where the Walk is agreeable even at Noon Day; but the common Mall as it may be called terminates about 1 Mile from the Town at a place called Montassy a little country retirement of the Governors. — Farther than this the Roads are wild and irregular. —

I may confine the Superior Class of Inhabitants to four Families and among those no European Women their dress therefore is not after our Fashion except in the Gown and Petticoat, and the first is only Worn at particular times the Common Bedgown being the General dress. — They Wear their Hair Combed Smooth back and formed in a Rose or Ring on the back of the Head secured by Diamond Pins and Combs richly Ornamented with Diamonds. — Their Complexion is fair in proportion as their removes are from the Malay Origin. — They use the Beetle and have gold and Silver Equipage for that use, but the Young Women do not Chew it publickly. — They are particularly Nice and Clean in their persons and some of them very pretty Women. —

Dancing is not common they have nevertheless a taste for Music and play very prettily on the Harp. — Ombre and Quinze fill up their vacant hours when they are disposed to visit, which with their parties in bathing and little excursions in the Country are all their amusements — But the life of this little community depends on the Governor, and perhaps no one was better calculated to dispense such blessings than the late Mr Van Este on whose Account this little Village may be said not to be in a Situation to have its Character justly drawn. —

Poultry Hogs and Goats are a Common property as likewise the Karrabow, but other horned Cattle and Sheep all that I saw belonged to the Governor. —

With respect to my Nautical remarks I can only say that the Island is about 64 leagues Long from SW to NE — the Island South point is in the latitude of 10..24 S° — I observed the latitude of Coupang to be 10..12 S° and from the Dutch Account the latitude of the NE and North End is 8..40 S° — From the same authority the Long° of Coupang is 121..51 East of Greenwich. this I may be able to ascertain hereafter by my run to Batavia. —

A large Island called Pulo Samow forms the Road of Coupang on the West. — it also extends round the West End of Timor and gives some secure situations in the West Monsoon, and the Anchorage is so extensive on each Side that numerous Fleets may Anchor in Safety. — Of course there are two Entrances into Coupang Road. Off the southernmost lies the Island Rotty to the SWBS. and in the Middle of the North Entrance is a Small Island surrounded by a Reef. which must be given a good birth to. — The North Entrance is the most elligible for Ships that are bound to Coupang. —

Wood and Water is always to be got here, but refreshments precarious,
it is however an elligible Stopping if Ships make Endeavor Streights a common pass
to and from Botany Bay. ——